Exploring Perceptions of Mentor Relationships in Doctoral Programs:

A Qualitative Exploratory Multiple-Case Study

by

Kenneth C. Jackson, D.M.

Copyright 2017©

Author	Kenneth C. Jackson, D.M., Wilmington, DE
Publisher	DBC Publishing, Virginia Beach, VA / Richmond, VA
ISBN	ISBN-13: 978-0692943588 ISBN-10: 0692943587
Cover Art	Copyright 2017© DBC Publishing
Copyright Notice	2016/2017©: All copyrights are reserved. The Author supports copyright, which encourages diverse viewpoints, promotes free speech, and creates a vibrant and rich academic culture. Thank you for buying an authorized copy of this copyrighted book and for complying with international copyright laws. You are supporting the author and academics to continue to publish. No part of this book, including interior design, cover design, icons, and/or pictures may be reproduced or transmitted in any form, by any means (electronic, photocopying, recording, or otherwise) without the prior written permission of the copyright owner. Independent of the author's economic rights, and even after the transfer of the said rights, the author shall have the right to claim authorship of the work and to object to any distortion, modification of, and/or other derogatory action in relation to the said work that could be deemed prejudicial to the author's honor or reputation. No part of this book or images – black and white, color, or other renditions of images, are to be posted to any social media, Internet, and/or other digital media or platforms without prior written permission of the copyright owner. Any actions taken by the reader in response to the book's contents shall be solely at their own risk. The author is waived of any legal or personal responsibility for anything that may happen due to readers taking actions after reading this book.
Trademarks	All brand names, product names, logos, service marks, trademarks or registered trademarks are trademarks of their respective owners.
Author:	You may contact the author with questions, comments, or continuing research inquiries at: kennethj42867@msn.com

A Dissertation Presented in Partial Fulfillment of the
Requirements for the Degree of

Doctor of Management in Organizational Leadership

University of Phoenix

The Dissertation Committee for Kenneth C. Jackson
certifies approval of the following dissertation:

**Exploring Perceptions of Mentor Relationships
in Doctoral Programs:
A Qualitative Exploratory Multiple-Case Study**

Marcia Hill, Ph.D. – Committee Chair
Terry Silver, Ed.D. – Committee Member
Patricia Shannon, Ph.D. – Committee Member
William C. Beck, II, Ph.D. – Academic Dean
School of Advanced Studies

Date Approved: December 11, 2016

TABLE OF CONTENTS

List of Tables 9
List of Figures 9
Abstract 11
Acknowledgements & Dedication 13
Chapter 1 15
    Introduction 15
    Background of the Problem 16
    Statement of the Problem 18
    Purpose of the Study 19
    Significance of the Study 20
        Significance of the Study to Leadership 21
        Significance of the Study to Management 22
        Nature of the Research Study 22
    Research Questions 26
    Theoretical Framework 27
        Mentor Relationship 28
        Interpersonal Relationship 28
        Traditional versus Non-traditional Mentoring 29
        Mentoring Relationship Impact 29
        Mentor Characteristics 30
        Cultural Influences 30
        Initiation 31
        Cultivation 31
        Separation 32
        Redefinition 32
        Social-Emotional Development 32
        Identity Development 33
        Cognitive Development 33
    Definition of Terms 34
    Assumptions 35
    Scope 35
    Limitations 36
    Delimitations 37
    Summary 38

Chapter 2 41
Review of the Literature 41
Historical Overview 41
Models of Mentoring 43
First Model 44
Initiation 44
Cultivation 45
Separation 45
Redefinition 46
Second Model 46
Social-emotional development 46
Identity development 48
Cognitive development 49
Conflicting Theories 50
Mentors at a Glance 52
Mentor Relationship Building 54
Compatibility 55
Time Investment 56
Lack of Support 57
Unclear Expectations 58
Trust 59
Interpersonal Relationship 60
Distance versus Traditional Doctoral Learning and Mentoring 61
Technology 62
Distance Learning 63
Traditional Learning 65
Negative and Positive Impact on Mentoring Relationships 67
Negative Impact 67
Attrition 67
Under-Achieving 68
Positive Impact 70
Mental attitude 71
Mentor Characteristics 72
Experience 72
Leadership 73
Communication 73
Self-Efficacy 74
Motivation 75
Emotional Intelligence 75
Moral Composition 76
Reputation 77
Cultural Influences 77
Mentoring Programs 78
Relevant Studies 79
Gap in Literature 85

Conclusion 88
Summary 89

Chapter 3 91
Method 91
Research Method and Design Appropriateness 91
    Research Method 91
Design Appropriateness 93
Research Questions 95
Population and Sampling 96
Informed Consent 97
Confidentiality 99
Data Collection 100
Field Test 102
Instrumentation 103
    Dependability, Credibility, and Transferability 104
    Dependability 105
    Credibility 106
    Transferability 107
Data Analysis 108
Summary 109

Chapter 4 111
Results 111
Data Collection Process 112
Field Test 112
    Changes to Field Test Interview Questions 113
Data Collection 116
Participant Coding 118
Demographic Information of Cases 119
    Years of Teaching Experience 119
    Years of Doctoral Mentoring Experience 119
    Ethnicity 120
    Age of Participants 120
Data Analysis 120
Emerging Themes 121
    Theme 1 – Cognitive Development 122
    Theme 2 – Matching Process 126
    Theme 3 – Indicators and Factors 130
    Theme 4 – Influence 133
    Theme 5 – Student Networking 135
    Theme 6 – Role 138
    Theme 7 – Relationships 141
    Theme 8 – Perceptions 144

    Theme 9 – Improvements 147
    Summary... 150

Chapter 5 .... **153**
    Conclusions and Recommendations 153
    Findings 153
        Theme 1. Cognitive Development 155
        Theme 2. Matching Process.. 155
        Theme 3. Indicators and Factors.. 156
        Theme 4. Influence... 157
        Theme 5. Student Networking 158
        Theme 6. Role.. 159
        Theme 7. Relationships.. 159
        Theme 8. Perceptions 160
        Theme 9. Improvements 161
    Limitations of the Study 162
    Delimitations of the Study 163
    Implications.. 164
    Implications to Leaders 166
        Significance to Leadership 167
        Recommendations for Leadership 168
        Recommendation for Future Research 169
    Conclusion 169

Appendices **171**
    Appendix A – Field Test Informed Consent Form..................... 173
    Appendix B – Informed Consent Form 177
    Appendix C – Letter of Invitation... 181
    Appendix D – Interview Questions.. 183
    Appendix E – Field Test Letter of Invitation.............................. 185
    Appendix F – Revision of Interview Questions 187

References **189**
Index **205**
Curriculum Vitae **211**
About The Author **221**
Contact The Author **222**
About The Book **224**

LIST OF TABLES

Table 1 - Erikson's Eight Stages of Development 47
Table 2 - Demographics 118
Table 3 - Frequency of Core Themes Mentioned by Participants 122

LIST OF FIGURES

Figure 1 - Frequency of responses and coverage percentages to cognitive development. References are the number of times participants spoke of or referenced cognitive development. Coverages are frequency percentages for the invariant constituents. 125
Figure 2 - Frequency of responses and coverage percentages to matching process. References are the number of times participants spoke of or referenced matching process. Coverages are frequency percentages for the invariant constituents. 130
Figure 3 - Frequency of responses and coverage percentages to indicators and factors. References are the number of times participants spoke of or referenced indicators and factors. Coverages are frequency percentages for the invariant constituents. 132
Figure 4 - Frequency of responses and coverage percentages to influence. References are the number of times participants spoke of or referenced influence. Coverages are frequency percentages for the invariant constituents. 135
Figure 5 - Frequency of responses and coverage percentages to student networking. References are the number of times participants spoke of or referenced student networking. Coverages are frequency percentages for the invariant constituents. 137

Figure 6 - Frequency of responses and coverage percentages to role. References are the number of times participants spoke of or referenced role. Coverages are frequency percentages for the invariant constituents. 141

Figure 7 - Frequency of responses and coverage percentages to relationships. References are the number of times participants spoke of or referenced relationships. Coverages are frequency percentages for the invariant constituents. 144

Figure 8 - Frequency of responses and coverage percentages to perceptions. References are the number of times participants spoke of or referenced perceptions. Coverages are frequency percentages for the invariant constituents. 147

Figure 9 - Frequency of responses and coverage percentages to improvements. References are the number of times participants spoke of or referenced improvements. Coverages are frequency percentages for the invariant constituents. 150

Abstract

The general problem researched in this study was the high attrition rate in doctoral programs across academic institutions. The specific problem was high attrition rates of doctoral students may be attributed to mentor/mentee relationships. The purpose of this qualitative, exploratory, multiple-case study was to explore mentoring relationships and student compatibility in doctoral programs. This design explained and gained an in-depth understanding of what creates a mentorship relationship for mentors and doctoral students.

Data collection for this qualitative research study was conducted through in-depth, open-ended, interview questions. Doctoral mentors shared their experiences and perceptions on mentoring doctoral students and expressed their experience with the mentoring process currently used at their perspective university.

Data analysis began with a goal of capturing themes and patterns within the interviews from study participants. Answers from the research participants was manually transcribed from a digital audio voice recorder and uploaded into NVivo 11 data analysis software and data was searched for themes and patterns. After analyzing each case, a cross-case analysis was used to identify overarching themes and patterns across each case. Common themes and patterns were identified until saturation was reached. Based on the data, nine emergent themes developed; (1) cognitive development, (2) matching process, (3) indicators and factors, (4) influence, (5) student networking, (6) role, (7) relationships, (8) perceptions, and (9) improvements.

The knowledge gained from this study attempted to assist institutional leaders focus on continuously developing effective strategies to help bridge the gap of failed mentoring relationships between doctoral candidates and their mentors.

Acknowledgements & Dedication

I acknowledge God and my Lord and Savior Jesus Christ, who has helped me through the good and challenging times of my doctoral journey. God has picked me up when I was down and helped lead me to this day in time. Without God, NONE of this would be possible.

I would like to acknowledge my family and friends who have shown their support throughout my doctoral journey. Many of you have stood beside me, and offered encouraging words of inspiration and motivation. You will never know how much your support meant to me and how it played a major role with the completion of my dissertation.

To my chair, Dr. Marcia Hill, who inspired me to work hard and to know hard work does pay off. Dr. Hill was instrumental with the success of my first-year residency. She provided the tools necessary to take this journey and to complete it, knowing she had my back. Dr. Hill never gave an easy way out and encouraged me to reach my full potential. I owe her a standing ovation.

To my committee members, Dr. Terry Silver and Dr. Patricia Shannon, who provided their professional scholarly expertise. Dr. Silver and Dr. Shannon were pivotal in my journey. They were my tour guides and never lead me off course.

I dedicate this dissertation to my wife, Tyra L. Jackson, who has pushed me from day one when I started my doctoral journey. When I felt like giving up, she was right there pushing me along and telling me I could do it. She gave me the motivation, inspiration, and the desire to complete my journey to the end. For that, I will forever be indebted, as she proved to be my rock, my foundation, and biggest supporter.

This dedication also goes out to my grandparents, Amelia Franco, Manual Franco, and Bessie Jackson, who are not here with us today. They are responsible for molding me into the man I am today. Without their teachings, I would not be in the position I am today. They were influential in my life; I know they are looking down with huge smiles on their faces.

Additionally, this dedication also belongs to my mother, Marilyn Jackson. She has provided me with the necessary tools to be successful in life, and taught me how to always strive for excellence. She taught me not to be afraid of trying; the way she raised me helped me become the man I am.

My father, Nathaniel Jackson, has been by my side and showed his support in more ways one can ever imagine. This dedication acknowledges the love I have for my father and shows him that his son is successful, giving him something of which to be proud.

My children, Kendra Jackson and Tyree Winfield, and my grandchildren, Eric Turner, and Ezra Washington, also deserve dedication … because I want them to see that hard work does pay off and to not to be afraid of going after their dreams. This shows them it can be done by using me as their model for motivation and inspiration.

Kenneth C. Jackson, D.M.

Chapter 1

Introduction

Mentoring relationships in doctoral programs can be a positive and necessary form of student development (Alderfer, 2014). Mentoring may be intense where developmental opportunities, counseling, and advice are provided to a mentee by a mentor due to personal or ethical conflicts (Pomeroy & Steiker, 2011). The majority of universities define the term mentoring similarly, yet mentoring relationships between doctoral mentors and students expand beyond immediate expectations of academic institutions (Goodyear, 2009).

Successful doctoral students develop a thorough understanding of the research process. Academic institutions may conceptualize the mentoring roles of doctoral chairs differently (Leshem, 2012). Doctoral mentors, which may consist of one or more individuals, may help develop academic writing and research abilities of doctoral students (Bryant-Shanklin & Brumage, 2011). Academic institutions' administrators and faculty stress the importance and value of mentoring through stimulating, positive-learning conditions (Mullen, 2007). Though gender and social status may play a role in these learning conditions, the doctoral mentor and student compatibility is important (Kent, Kochan, & Green, 2013). Academic institutions must recognize diverse cultural backgrounds between mentors and mentees (also referred to as protégés) to assist in effectively matching the pair (Zozakiewicz, 2010).

Chapter 1 includes background information on mentoring relationships between doctoral students and doctoral mentors. The background information served as the basis for further description on the general and specific problems investigated in this study.

The purpose and significance of the study, in terms of how doctoral mentors perceive the mentoring relationship experience and student compatibility in doctoral programs, followed the statement of the problem. An explanation of the nature of the study that focused on the study's method and case study design was identified. A theoretical framework which focused on mentoring and student compatibility was also described.

Background of the Problem

Doctoral mentors' and doctoral students' mentoring relationships are an important factor for quality educational experiences (Lechuga, 2011). University mentoring processes are important and meeting mentees' psychosocial and academic needs may be instrumental by understanding developmental stages and assessing mentee capabilities (Pomeroy & Steiker, 2011). Mentors and mentees possessing psychosocial development may help mentoring relationships become more compatible by providing a clear identity and a sense of competence (May-Chiun Lo & Ramayah, 2011). Hellsten, Prytula, Ebanks, and Lai (2009) established compatibility as an important element to the mentor/mentee relationship.

Various theoretical domains exist between mentors and mentees as they build a mutual relationship. The psychosocial domains may consist of skills and qualities in developing interpersonal relationships (Yob & Crawford, 2012). According to Yob and Crawford, other psychosocial domains may consist of the attitudes and values in building and sustaining mentoring relationships. Some attributes that may emerge from doctoral chairs include the coach, sponsor, and mentor (Alderfer, 2014).

Mentoring has been the focus of attention in many universities and may be a contributing factor helping doctoral students in completing doctoral programs (Malmgren, Ottino, & Amaral, 2010). Research on mentoring has taken center stage in academic institutions, and researchers have recognized existing variations in student satisfaction levels obtained through mentoring relationships (Belle, Cotton, & Miller, 2000). Implementing poor mentoring processes negatively impacts mentees' relational experience with their mentors (Brill & McCartney, 2008). Mentoring programs – poorly established – may facilitate more stress, lower expectations for faculty members, and mentees may experience burn-out as a result of an ineffectual and improperly trained mentor (Smethem, 2007). Mentees experiencing poorly established mentoring programs may find their only choice is to drop out of the doctoral program.

The roles of faculty members in academic institutions traditionally include teaching, scholarship, and service with some degree of mentoring embedded in all three roles (Zipp, Cahill, & Clark, 2009), which may be beneficial to effective mentoring. Academic leadership also face challenges that provide unclear direction in the mentoring process (Malmgren et al., 2010). Benefits of effective mentoring relationships may result in positive career success and positive attitudes pertaining to degree completion (Wang, Tomlinson, & Noe, 2010). Mentors and mentees portraying positive elements of the relationship, and whom actively contribute to the mentoring relationship, may help doctoral students more successfully through the academic journey. At the same time, differences in cultural backgrounds may present challenges in producing positive attitudes in mentoring relationships (Holley & Caldwell, 2012).

Understanding the role of mentorship in doctoral programs can lead to enhancement of the program and can also increase the productivity of students and faculty (Zipp et al., 2009). As enhancements are placed at the forefront of effective mentoring, doctoral programs must acknowledge cultural differences in mentoring relationships. Academic institutions may create a mindset that certain mentees always need assistance and are dependent on others to reach academic goals (Kent et al., 2013). Socialization of respective disciplinary cultures is important when establishing relationships between mentor and mentee (Lechuga, 2011).

Statement of the Problem

The general problem is a high attrition rate in doctoral programs across academic institutions (Holley & Caldwell, 2012). About 50% of doctoral students drop out without finishing (Di Pierro, 2012). Doctoral students often face negative consequences, such as a feeling of failure, due to attrition rates at the university in doctoral programs (Willis & Carmichael, 2011). Mentors and mentees who have not taken time to get to know each other in a professional and/or academic setting can experience negative consequences resulting from poor communication, personality conflicts, and strained relationships (Bell & Treleaven, 2011). Academic institutions are focusing on retaining doctoral students due to half the doctoral student population dropping out of doctoral programs (Di Pierro, 2012). Attrition rates not only have the potential of negatively affecting the universities by having lack of student enrollments in doctoral programs, but can possibly have a negative effect on the student because the student may feel unsupported throughout a doctoral program (Hovdhaugen, 2011). Universities utilizing more resources to improve mentoring relationship and student compatibility efforts gain more student trust in the mentoring process.

This qualitative exploratory multiple-case research studied doctoral mentors' perceptions on their roles of mentoring and the student's compatibility with their mentor in doctoral programs. The specific problem studied was high attrition rates of doctoral students that may be attributed to mentor/mentee relationships.

Attrition rates for students in doctoral programs occur at different stages and mentor/mentee incompatibility may be present in any stage (Harris, 2011). Doctoral students that drop out at a certain stage of the doctoral program may rarely be provided the proper resources and guidance to complete the doctoral program (O'Meara, Knudsen, & Jones, 2013). When doctoral mentors are poorly qualified to guide students, it may prevent students from completing dissertations (Ewing, Mathieson, Alexander, & Leafman, 2012).

Purpose of the Study

The purpose of this exploratory, multiple-case research study was to explore doctoral mentors' perceptions on mentoring relationship experiences and student compatibility between mentors and mentees in doctoral programs. This research study involved 10 doctoral mentors who mentor doctoral students from two different universities in the state of Delaware. The results of this study may provide provosts, academic deans, and doctoral chairs information they can use to evaluate and improve the mentoring process in doctoral programs.

Electing to conduct a qualitative research study helps researchers produce a higher level of detailed information from a smaller sample of research participants (Patton, 1990). According to Babbi (2004), detailed information from qualitative studies is rich in meaning that also provides superior validity, and strives to gain an intimate, firsthand knowledge of the research setting, but simultaneously is careful not to be too distant from the participants being studied (Neuman, 2011).

A case-study design was appropriate for exploring doctoral mentors' perceptions on mentoring relationship experiences and student compatibility in doctoral programs. The multiple-case, study design was also appropriate for this study to conduct a causal investigation and the existence of how questions make the study appropriate (Tellis, 1997; Yin, 1994). The existence of how questions were used to view a variety of perspectives allowed multiple facets of perceptions to be captured (Baxter & Jack, 2008).

Significance of the Study

The significance of this qualitative, exploratory, multiple-case study was to provide insight into the perceptions of doctoral mentors' roles to assist higher education leaders, working in conjunction with business leaders, to prepare mentoring programs for effective business manager leaders (O'Dell, 1990). Doctoral students may experience or perceive a lack of support, which could be the result of a failed mentor/mentee relationship. The failure in properly supporting prospective mentors with necessary skills to become effective mentors may fail when mentoring relationships are neglected

(Martin, 2002). Institutional leaders may be able to provide improved or realigned mentorship practices and/or training addressing doctoral students learning needs, thus possibly increasing doctoral student completion rates.

This qualitative study may assist institutional leaders in developing strategies for effective mentoring relationships. The research study may also assist management in making policy and procedural changes in areas that need change. The results of this study may be transferable to doctoral mentor programs to assist program completion for business manager leaders. The results may provide academic leaders new or added insights for building effective mentorship relationships between doctoral mentors and doctoral mentees.

Significance of the Study to Leadership

Mentoring plays a significant role for doctoral students pursuing doctoral degrees and for transitioning into leadership roles (Myers, 2012). Mentoring occurs for personal and professional purposes, but also for leadership purposes (Laughlin & Moore, 2012). Not until the late 1980s did mentoring literature and research refer to developing leadership (Campbell, Smith, Dugan, & Komives, 2012). Until then, leadership was labeled as a derivative of successful development of mentoring relationships (Campbell et al., 2012). Scholar leaders began linking mentoring and leadership behaviors as a mean to influence mentee's capacity level for leadership (Campbell et al., 2012).

Mentors who are unwilling to share specific experiences or learned skills may not be effective leaders to mentees, which may prevent mentees from developing into leaders. When mentors are willing to share experiences, and offer constructive opinions, mentees reach goals more confidently (Hamlin & Sage, 2011; Wahat, Jrauss, & Othman, 2013). Mentees that reach goals and become more confident with themselves make effective leaders. Confident doctoral mentees may become effective doctoral mentors to others, proving the ability to lead others.

Significance of the Study to Management

The significance of this exploratory, multiple-case study to management was to identify different dimensions of the mentoring relationship experiences that doctoral mentors described as being personally successful in leadership positions. As a leader, doctoral mentors manage how students are mentored. Many professions, such as community leaders, sports coaches, and educators, utilize mentoring services to empower (protégés) individuals. This research study may benefit management professions' current mentoring policies and procedures within business organizations. Organizational management may use authority for problem solving and changing mentoring processes to ensure mentors are effectively building positive mentoring relationships with mentees (Prevodnik & Biloslavo, 2009). Understanding the dynamics and outcomes of this research study may help professional managers evaluate current mentoring policies and procedures to ensure placement of effective mentoring practices.

Nature of the Research Study

The goal of this qualitative, exploratory, multiple-case study was to have research participants identify what constitutes a successful mentoring relationship between doctoral mentors and doctoral students. This qualitative study involved accumulating, examining, and interpreting data based on participants' mentoring relationship experiences as a doctoral mentor. Before the research portion of this study could begin, a field test was conducted by selecting two doctoral mentors from two universities. Interview questions were analyzed and tested by field test participants for validity, reliability, adequacy, and to allow the formation of the final interview questions.

Participants selected for the field test were not used in the follow-on, qualitative, multiple-case study research study. The actual research study focused on 10 doctoral mentors from two universities in the state of Delaware. Data was collected using in-depth interviews and strategized by using purposeful sampling (Baxter & Jack, 2008). Incorporating purposeful sampling provides the study with more credibility, trustworthiness, and overall quality (Baxter & Jack, 2008). The data collected from participants represented individual perceptions describing the experiences of establishing mentoring relationships.

The perceptions of doctoral mentors' experiences of mentoring doctoral students and student compatibility was explored. This qualitative research method best aligns with the research problem and research questions presented. Study participants were investigated in a natural environmental setting, and the researcher collected multiple types of subjective data (Denzin & Lincoln, 1994). According to Stein and Mankowski (2004), qualitative research applies a process of identifying the participants and obtaining data on participants' experiences. Data was interpreted and made accessible to community researchers after collection (Stein & Mankowski, 2004).

This qualitative, exploratory, research study included an interpretive approach to evaluate the participants' perspectives in a semi-structured interview process. An interpretive approach enabled participants to respond to interview questions to generate themes and patterns associated with mentoring relationships with doctoral students (Leedy & Ormrod, 2010). According to Patton (1990), data obtained through interviews are consistent with qualitative research. The analysis of this data was the basis for searching for themes found in qualitative data instead of variables associated with quantitative data (Neuman, 2011).

    Conducting a quantitative research examined the problem and quantifies findings from the obtained data (Bloomberg & Volpe, 2008). According to Bloomberg and Volpe (2008), variables were first identified in quantitative research and then hypotheses were created. Evidence found in quantitative research would or would not support the hypotheses.

    In conducting a qualitative research, variables are not present and hypotheses did not have to be identified. The results of this qualitative research study were interpreted and not quantified, as with quantitative research; therefore, a qualitative, exploratory, multiple-case study was appropriate to explore perceptions of doctoral mentors' experiences of mentoring doctoral students and student compatibility.

    A case study was the most appropriate for this research study to explore how or why doctoral mentors' experiences of mentoring students and student compatibility may have affected business leaders' completion of their doctoral programs (Yin, 2014). The over-arching research question for this qualitative, exploratory, multiple-case study was 'how do doctoral mentors perceive the role of mentoring and student compatibility in doctoral programs?' The perceptions and experiences of doctoral mentors with no perceived, clear, or single outcome was explored and was the best strategy when answering interview questions in case study designs (Yin, 2003).

A multiple-case, study design was appropriate for this exploratory study as the rationale included the ability to access more information of doctoral mentors' perceptions that was previously inaccessible, thus making the study worth conducting (Yin, 2014). In multiple-case studies, the differences between cases was explored and this study involved case findings between two different universities the researcher tried to replicate across each case. Comparisons was drawn from five doctoral mentors at each of the two universities and explored the results across the different cases as a goal to predict similar or contrasting results (Yin, 2003). The study was descriptive and provided inductive views of each participants mentoring experience. This multiple-case study explored differences and similarities between participants by collecting data through an informal manner.

Interviews were one of the main sources of case study evidence. Open-ended, interview questions relating to the mentor-mentee relationship experiences enabled participants to provide in-depth personal perceptions. Case study interviews may focus directly on the case, which may provide insightful explanations and perceptions; similar to guided conversations (Yin, 2014). Conducting interviews was an important element in case study design as the majority of case studies dealt with actions or affairs of human behavior (Baxter & Jack, 2008). Participants selected for this multiple-case, study research provided instrumental insight into doctoral mentor/mentee relationships (Yin, 2014).

Common themes and patterns on doctoral mentors' perceptions of the mentoring role and student compatibility were examined. Answers from the research participants were transcribed from a digital, audio, voice-recorder and uploaded into a data analysis software. NVivo was the primary data analysis tool to review, analyze, and interpret the collected data. NVivo is a computer-based, data analysis tool used in qualitative research to analyzing contents and enhance the data analysis process from the responses of the interview with participants (NVivo, 2013). NVivo11 was used for the coding and analysis of the text and audio results from the interview with the 10 doctoral mentors from two different Delaware universities.

After analyzing each case, a cross-case analysis was used to identify the overarching themes and patterns across each case. A cross-case analysis consisted of investigating and analyzing themes and patterns. Researchers using cross-case analysis helped identify similarities and differences about each case and these cases were reviewed to develop themes and patterns (Stake, 2006). Stake's (2006) cross-case analysis procedure consisted of reviewing each case from collected data to identify prominent themes and patterns. NVivo grouped phrases and words creating common themes and patterns to discover terms frequently used from the interviews. The emerging themes from NVivo were coded in different categories to ensure manageability of major themes. According to Morse (1995), saturation is reached when no new information can be obtained from qualitative data, therefore common themes and patterns were identified until saturation was reached.

Research Questions

Findings from 10 doctoral mentors from two Delaware universities were analyzed and reported. The questions presented to selected participants were open-ended, which had a direct reflection on the purpose statement: to explore doctoral mentors' perceptions on mentoring relationship experiences and student compatibility in doctoral programs. Participants answering the open-ended questions helped develop conversational tones that led to participants telling stories of experiences while mentoring doctoral students.

The qualitative multiple-case study focused on one central question and two sub-questions. The research question was, as follows:

R1: How do doctoral mentors perceive the role of student mentoring and student compatibility in doctoral programs?

The following sub-questions guided the development of this qualitative research study and provided a foundation for developing the interview questions for the participants:

S1: How do doctoral mentors perceive the importance of the initiation phase of a mentor/mentee relationship?

S2: How do doctoral mentors perceive the importance of mentee cognitive development during the mentor/mentee relationship?

Theoretical Framework

Doctoral mentors' perceptions on the role of mentoring students and student compatibility in doctoral programs was examined. Frameworks and theories exist for understanding background factors governing doctoral mentors' perception on the role of mentoring. Theoretical frameworks guiding this qualitative study included the role of mentors and mentees when building a mentoring relationship. Major models of mentoring drive this research study and one such model includes Kram's (1983) mentoring cycle, which consists of initiation, cultivation, separation, and redefinition. Another model driving this research study consisted of social-emotional development, identity development, and cognitive development. Mentors and mentees formed an understanding of the mentoring relationship in terms of characteristics, traits, and environmental influences when establishing theoretical frameworks and using various mentoring models.

Mentor Relationship

Challenges may be faced when mentors and mentees build a mentoring relationship where mentors show insufficient support for the mentee (Kahle-Piasecki, 2011). Some identified challenges were compatibility, time-investment, lack of support, unclear expectations, and lack of trust. These negative experiences can be found throughout academic institutions where a formal mentoring process is lacking (the entire process was lacking or simply inefficient or ineffectual) (Kahle-Piasecki, 2011). Mentors should carry out mentoring actions with a goal in mind and understand, to be effective, mentoring must be intentional (Smith, 2005). When the relationship is built intentionally, both the mentor and mentee are fully engaged with one another (Smith, 2005).

Interpersonal Relationship

William Schutz developed the Fundamental Interpersonal Relations Orientation Behavior (FIRO-B) theory of interpersonal relations (Schutz, 1958). FIRO-B theory indicates there were three basic interpersonal needs accounting for interpersonal behavior, which included inclusion, control, and affection (Siegel, Smith, & Mosca, 2001). A person's social orientation was associated with the inclusion aspect of FIRO-B, indicating a need for interacting and a sense of belonging (Siegel et al., 2001). The affection FIRO- B area referred to intimacy needs of a person and friendship which builds compatibility (Siegel et al., 2001). The type of affection needed will vary from one individual to another (Siegel et al., 2001). The last behavior area under Schultz's basic interpersonal needs was control related to power and influence (Siegel et al., 2001).

Traditional versus Non-traditional Mentoring

Doctoral students who attended non-traditional education, through online classes, experience frustration and negative emotions with distant social relationships with mentors, which may lead to incompatibility (Saade & Kira, 2007). It could be difficult to adjust to the lack of face-to-face interactions in the mentoring relationship. The most popular choice in relationship building continues to be traditional mentoring in an academic setting (Mavrinac, 2005). Having a non-traditional mentoring relationship can increase the risk of miscommunication opposed to face-to-face interaction where communication levels are understood more clearly (Whiting & de Janasz, 2004).

Mentoring Relationship Impact

Mentors and mentees may have had different perspectives that influence the mentoring relationships outcome (Toby, 2005). A variety of internal and external influences in mentoring relationships may have produced negative outcomes. Internal and external influences could also have produced positive outcomes. Negative impacts could have consisted of attrition rates, students underachieving, stress, and incompatibility. Positive impacts could have consisted of high academic performance, interpersonal confidence, and positive mental attitudes.

Mentor Characteristics

Mentors that effectively guided mentees in completing doctoral degrees without dropping out or prolonging graduation efforts possessed certain types of interpersonal traits and characteristics (Johnson, 2002). Some traits that influenced the progression of doctoral students were embedded in the mentor's experience, leadership, communication skills, self-efficacy, motivational skills, Emotional Intelligence (EI), moral composition, and reputation. Considering these skills, mentors should be able to match internal qualities that were compatible to mentees when building mentoring relationships (Wang & Fulton, 2012).

Cultural Influences

Mentoring doctoral students can take on different styles because of diverse cultural backgrounds of the mentor and student. Past research on successful mentoring relationships show mentors are culturally aware and sensitive to mentees' needs (Kent et al., 2013). The cultural aspects pertaining to building a mentoring relationship was essential to overcoming obstacles to success (Blickle, Schneider, Meurs, & Perrewé, 2010). Doctoral students may have become unmotivated when there is a lack of cultural compatibility (Yamauchi, 1998).

Initiation

Building a mentoring relationship was ideal in supporting doctoral students' needs; some students did not progress any further than the initiation phase (Anne Bogat, Liang, & Rigol-dahn, 2008). The initiation phase of the mentoring relationship was where mentees fantasize about doctoral mentors providing support and guidance to complete the doctoral program (Kram, 1983). Few doctoral students making it through the initiation phase may have had the potential feeling of dropping out (of the program) due to a mentor's unresolved frustration with the mentee (Anne Bogat, Liang, & Rigol-dahn, 2008). Mentors must possess a warm and inviting attitude in the acquaintance phase for the initiation to have been successful in reaching the cultivation phase.

Cultivation

During the cultivation phase, doctoral students started to acknowledge growth and a sense of competence with themselves and the mentoring relationship (Kram, 1983), resulting in mentees navigating through the doctoral program more effectively (Kram, 1983). The mentors' ability to cultivate becomes empowering for the mentee to get through the doctoral program (Sugimoto, 2012b). Mentees became more confident with the level of knowledge and the guidance received which prepared mentees for separation from their mentor.

Separation

During the separation phase, mentees may start to feel a sense of anxiety, a sense of feeling lost, and turmoil because the mentoring relationship started to diminish (Kram, 1983). Mentors may have felt guidance was no longer adequate to support mentees. Mentees may have also felt more independent or may have come to the end of the doctoral journey with a mentor. The separation phase often lessened the emotional attachment in the mentoring relationship (Eby, Butts, Lockwood, & Simon, 2004).

Redefinition

After the separation phase, doctoral mentors and students may redefine roles. These roles may include building a friendship or collaborating on projects together although feelings of superiority and/or inequality levels may still exist (Kram, 1983). Because a hierarchy level still exists in this phase, hostility can set in where mentors and mentees may face resentment with one another (Sugimoto, 2012b). It is important to establish boundaries early in this stage to prevent any friction.

Social-Emotional Development

Mentees strongly engaging with mentors and building a strong connection may increase their own ability to identify with others (Rhodes, Grossman, & Resch, 2000). As doctoral mentors and students meet for the first time, different elements are brought into the relationship consisting of physical, emotional, and social characteristics (Rubin, 1998). The interactions in the relationship will vary due to each person's social situation and each other's personal characteristics (Rubin, 1998). Developing the social and emotional aspect may be complex, but both parties must understand each other's disposition to have an effective relationship.

Identity Development

By being a role model, doctoral mentors have a significant contribution to doctoral students' identity development (Rhodes et al., 2006). An important element of a students' identity development is the process of establishing a good working relationship with doctoral mentors (Russell & Horne, 2009). A close-working relationship should counteract stereotypical thinking that mentoring relationship may not be successful in doctoral programs. A great deal of support from mentors enables the students' self- confidence and self-esteem (Struthers, 1995). Doctoral students that feel this sense of confidence and self-esteem may find the doctoral journey much easier to achieve, which prevents the student from dropping out of the program.

Cognitive Development

Mentors and mentees that create positive mentoring relationships may help contribute to a mentees' cognitive development by exposing the mentees to new learning patterns, providing intellectual guidance, and promoting academic success (Rhodes et al., 2006). Strategies established with cognitive development enhances an individuals' ability to acquire and apply new knowledge learned (Hezlett, 2005). Some of these strategies may include what students already know and how students can self-regulate the thought and learning processes (Hezlett, 2005). Students start to create a new way of thinking and learning which is important for dissertation research.

Definition of Terms

The following is a list of terms used in the context of this research study:

Interpersonal relationship, as defined by Liu, Yin, and Huang (2013), is a developmental process where people share with one another, building trust and value under mutual interaction.

Leadership development is a type of human development process that takes place over time (Olivares, 2008). This active and developmental process seeks to enhance member's productive capacity through a goal inspired relationship (Olivares, 2008).

Mentee is one who is being mentored; also known as a protégé (Mentee, 2014).

Mentors are experienced individuals that invest time and effort to guide, nurture, assist, and develop those less experienced (Rekha & Ganesh, 2012).

Mentor Relationship is a relationship built over time between two individuals, where one consists of a less experienced person (mentee or protégé), and an experienced individual as the mentor (Price & McMullan, 2012). Within this relationship, the mentor provides guidance, practical help, and consistent support (Price & McMullan, 2012).

Assumptions

This qualitative research study contained several assumptions of the participants of the study: doctoral mentors. The assumption was all doctoral mentors were familiar and knowledgeable with the mentoring process. The second assumption was participants represented a group of individuals able to provide multiple perspectives on the mentoring process in associated academic institutions. The presumption was participants were providing their best and honest answers to interview questions, while sharing mentoring relationship experiences in a doctoral program. Participants were provided a supportive and private area to conduct the interview. After participants felt comfortable, there were no issue with providing open and honest answers to interview questions. The third assumption was participants selected have worked as a mentor for at least three years to obtain enough relatable information on participants' experiences. The final assumption was interview questions were clear and each participant understood what was being asked.

Scope

The scope of the study was limited to exploring doctoral mentors' perceptions on mentoring relationship experiences along with student compatibility while matriculating a doctoral program. The population for this qualitative research study consisted of 10 doctoral mentors who mentored or were mentoring doctoral students from two different universities in the state of Delaware. Five mentors from each university were drawn randomly from each university's faculty database. A qualitative case study research design provided an opportunity by using open-ended interview questions to elicit the perceptions and experiences of doctoral mentors pertaining to mentoring relationships.

Limitations

The limitations in research study are matters and potential weaknesses uncontrollable by the researcher, and that may potentially influence the direction of the study (Christensen, Johnson, & Turner, 2011). This study had various limitations that could have affected the completion of the study. Using a case study approach may fail to accurately report findings (Yin, 2003). Thick description of the case gave proper understanding of the case. Data were collected through a structured interview using open-ended questions being tape-recorded and transcribed.

A second limitation was time management and limited availability of participants. Scheduling demands of participants and professional work demands limited the findings of the study. Participants were given a variety of time slots and dates to choose from to meet the needs of the study. Date and times were provided in advance for participants to choose a mutually beneficial date and time.

A third limitation was the honesty and openness of participants when answering interview questions. Participants being truthful about personal experiences and perceptions may feel responses could have led to a reprimand from leadership at the academic institution. To deal with this limitation, participants were provided a supportive and confidential location for the interview to take place. Participants were told verbally (and within the informed consent form; see Appendices A and B) all information obtained would be kept in strict confidence. Each participant's name and university remained confidential and known only to the researcher. To ensure anonymity and confidentiality, each university and participant had an alpha-numeric code for use within the audio recording and transcript. Selected codes were used in place of the individuals' name and the selected university. After presenting participants with the confidentiality plan, there were no issues with the participants answering the interview questions truthfully and honestly.

A fourth limitation was potential researcher bias when collecting data and interpreting the data (Patton, 2001). Prejudices and personal views were explored prior to interviewing participants through bracketing. Preconceptions about the research study before data was collected, analyzed, and interpreted were set aside from the participants' responses (Al-Natour, Qandil, & Gillespie, 2015). Researchers may have an emotional relationship with the research topic and these emotions must be protected from skewing data (Tufford & Newman, 2010). Researchers were in a position to see the study through the eyes of each participant, which also alleviated social desirability bias. Finally, the fifth limitation was the transferability of participants' responses. Open-ended interview questions facilitated one-on-one discussions promoting in-depth responses. Accurate coding and categorization during the data analysis was strictly followed to promote in-depth responses.

Delimitations

The delimitations of a research study are aspects a researcher can control, set boundaries, or limit (Leedy & Ormrod, 2010). Delimitations narrowed the scope by exploring perceptions of experienced doctoral mentors who currently mentor doctoral students from two universities in the state of Delaware that included male and female participants. A second delimitation narrowed the research study down to doctoral mentors that have been in the mentoring role for over three years. A purposeful sample of male and female doctoral mentors were used. The interview questions were limited to inquiry about the doctoral mentors' perceptions of the mentoring experience and did not include questions about religion or cultural beliefs.

Summary

Mentoring has become the center of attention in many organizations, and the momentum continues to grow as mentor relationships form (Ragins & Kram, 2009). The general appeal mentoring has is the transformational relationship formed between the mentor and mentee (Ragins & Kram, 2009). Past mentoring literature have different views on what constitutes an effective mentoring relationship, which finds mentors and mentees perceptions of effective mentoring quite different (Elizabeth, Bhave, & Kyoung, 2012). Mentoring relationships are important for doctoral students, because doctoral students are potential ambassadors to the respective field of study (Becher, 1989). A lack of understanding of what constitutes a successful mentorship relationship can potentially have a negative impact on the mentoring relationship.

The purpose of this exploratory, multiple-case study was to explore doctoral mentors' perceptions on mentoring relationship experiences and student compatibility in doctoral programs. This study involved 10 doctoral mentors who mentor doctoral students from two different universities in the state of Delaware. Chapter 2 provided an in-depth discussion of literature, conceptual frameworks and theories existing on mentoring relationships, and current research discoveries on mentoring and building a mentoring relationship between mentors and mentees.

Chapter 2

Review of the Literature

The purpose of this exploratory, multiple-case study was to explore doctoral mentors' perceptions on mentoring relationship experiences and student compatibility in doctoral programs. This study focused on doctoral mentors from two universities in the state of Delaware. The primary focus of this qualitative study was on doctoral mentors mentoring relationship experiences. Chapter 2 includes a historical overview and comprehensive review of literature on mentoring and building a mentoring relationship between mentors and mentees.

Historical Overview

Various sources provide a definition for mentoring: dictionaries, encyclopedias, Internet sources, faculty leaders, and academic leaders. The term mentor can be traced to ancient Greek mythology and described in Homer's *The Odyssey* where Mentor, a friend of Odysseus, was seen as a designated authority figure (Wright, 1992). Mentor was noted as being a smart and benevolent counselor chosen by Athena, the Goddess of Wisdom (Whitney, 2004). Mentor established himself as being a man with character, directness, and most of all, integrity (Koocher, 2002). The capacity mentoring played during this historic period and literature work focused on life instead of the narrowed capacity mentoring is used for today (Lorentzon & Brown, 2003; Marriott, 2006).

A group of social scientists in 1978, headed by Daniel Levinson, published *The Seasons of a Man's Life*, which explored the lives of 40 men building a mentoring relationship and indicated the important role mentors play in an individual's life, serving as the more experienced individual over the inexperienced nature of the protégé. According to Barondess (1995), the mentors were in the role of teacher, advisor, and sponsor. Mentors, through teaching, guide protégés to enhance skills and scholarly development. In the advisory role, mentors provide moral support, personal counseling, and guidance, while sponsors influenced mentees in future advancements in the field of choice (Barondess, 1995).

Shortly after Levinson's literature, Kathy Kram published *Mentoring at Work*, which provided an understanding and theoretical foundation on mentoring relationships between men and women and defined the theoretical construct of mentoring. According to Ragins and Kram (2009), once the construct of mentoring was defined, research on mentoring increased. Results from the multitude of research started moving the mentoring concept from an academic construct to a broader construct including communities, businesses, and households.

The original traditional means of mentoring was defined as an older person with more experience building a relationship with a less experienced younger individual (Ragins & Kram, 2007). The relationship built between older and younger individuals was established to help develop the career of the younger individual (Kram, 1985). Mentoring began to provide two types of functions in assisting mentees: career and psychosocial functions (Kram, 1985). Psychosocial functions are established by building a bond and trust with one another. Psychosocial functions focus on mentoring academic relationships when doctoral students are pursuing a doctoral degree.

Mentoring is more than providing advice to a protégé and includes the process of building a one-to-one relationship with a mentee (Gay, 1994). A goal for developing trusting mentor/mentee relationships exceeds a transfer of knowledge (Gay, 1994). Faculties have felt an increased pressure to enhance productivity, since the retrenchment conditions of the early 1970s through most of the 1980s (Williams & Blackburn, 1988). To enhance and improve faculty productivity, educational institutions responded with the use of mentoring (Williams & Blackburn, 1988).

Doctoral student mentoring includes a long history of mentoring doctoral students in education where mentors guide students through research study, helping network with professionals, and assist students in meeting educational goals (Anderson & Shore, 2008; Davis, 2007; Forehand, 2008; Hu, Thomas, & Lance, 2008, Paglis, Green, & Bauer, 2006). Mentoring is meant to provide a positive, nourishing, and constructive basis for mentees' achievements. Doctoral students can spend more than three years pursuing a doctorate degree and may experience difficult times throughout the journey. Many academic institutions are requiring new faculty members to have a doctorate degree, which enhances faculty members in a positive and rewarding way (Fedler, 1996). Faculty members mentor doctoral students pursuing doctorate degrees and the professional relationship may extend outside of the classroom (Tice, 1996).

Models of Mentoring

A key component for doctoral students' educational development and personal growth is through mentoring.

Doctoral mentors use mentoring models and strategies to develop and promote mentees' abilities in completing doctoral programs (Delaney, 2012). Different mentoring models used in mentoring relationships provide different levels of support (Hallam, Chou, Hite, & Hite, 2012). Depending on a students' personal characteristic make-up, doctoral mentors choose the model that best fits the needs of the mentoring relationship. Kram's theory and model of mentoring consist of initiation, cultivation, separation, and redefinition. Another model facilitating pathways of mentor influence is through social-emotional development, identity development, and cognitive development.

First Model

Initiation. Doctoral students face a challenging road when deciding to pursue a doctoral degree. Having a mentor helps guide the student through different phases of the doctoral journey; building a positive relationship is important. Mentors and mentees must have a starting point when establishing a mentoring relationship. According to Kram (1983), the starting point is considered the initiation phase where expectations are set for the relationship, should be met with mutual engagement, and (the initiation period) can last up to one year (Wu, Turban, & Cheung, 2012).

Doctoral mentors should be available to mentees when needed, which is part of setting the initial expectations. Mentors that begin with a respectful, friendly, and responsive attitude tend to build strong mentoring relationships (Dreyer, 2014). At this stage, mentors and mentees can tell if the relationship will be a good fit. Bozeman and Feeney (2008) constructed a theoretical model that studied the 'Goodness of Fit' in the mentoring relationship. The theory behind fit was how well individual abilities, attributes, and needs were matched between mentors and mentees (Lunsford, 2011). If these elements matched well, it would potentially lead to a positive mentoring relationship.

Cultivation. At some period in a positive mentoring relationship, mentees begin to grow and evolve. The mentee functions almost independently from positive engagement with mentors. Kram suggested this model of mentoring is the cultivation phase (Kiran, Majumdar, & Kishore, 2012). The relationship established starts to build a stronger bond and the expansion of the mentoring functions start widening. The mentee starts to operate more effectively while trying to achieve new or ongoing goals and objectives.

The cultivation phase in the mentoring relationship can last anywhere from two to five years (Robinson & Reio, 2012). Mentees begin to grow in this stage and acquire more knowledge. The knowledge gained is through various opportunities presented by the mentor in the relationship (Fragoulis, Valkanos, & Voula, 2011). At this phase of the mentoring cycle, mentors offer comfort and support while mentees continue to grow (Schunk & Mullen, 2013). It is at this cultivation phase where the benefit of mentoring occurs.

Separation. Mentoring relationships will change over time and, at some point, the mentor and mentee will part ways. Mentees may feel equipped to separate from the mentor to complete tasks and accomplish goals (Khosla, 2013). The theory behind the separation phase is mentees are now capable of working independently. The separation phase could also be a point where mentors and mentees are no longer able to work cohesively together due to contradictory feelings or attitudes. The process of separation begins the psychological disengagement between mentors and mentees (Kiran et al., 2012). After the separation phase, the mentoring relationship enters the redefinition phase.

Redefinition. During the mentoring relationship, mentors and mentees could maximize the experience of the relationship, which helps mentees develop positive results (Washington, 2011). Once the relationship reaches success from both parties the mentor / mentee relationship enters Kram's final mentoring model phase called redefinition (Popoola, Adesopo, & Ajayi, 2013). The redefinition phase is where mentors ideally continue to be supporters, but on a different level than previously established in the relationship. Pertaining to doctoral students, this psychosocial element is established once the student graduates and is formally separated from mentors (Sugimoto, 2012a). At this point mentors' role and purpose to the mentee is as a friend, peer, and/or colleague.

Second Model

Social-emotional development. Social emotional development plays an important role in doctoral mentoring relationships because different mentees have different personalities. Young adults go through a psychosocial development stage and according to environmental or social factors each adolescent may progress differently (Phipps, 2011). Individuals will go through a social and emotional identity development progressing through different stages of life (Rausch, 2012). Social emotional development is considered a socialization process that theorist Erik Erikson illustrates as eight developmental stages (Phipps, 2011) (see table 1).

Table 1 - Erikson's Eight Stages of Development

Stage	Social-Emotional Development	Personality	Learning Time-period (Age)
1	Basic Trust versus Mistrust	Hope	Infancy up to two years old
2	Autonomy versus Shame	Will	2 to 4 years old
3	Initiative versus Guilt	Purpose	4 to 5 years old
4	Industry versus Inferiority	Competence	5 to 12 years old
5	Identity versus Identity Diffusion	Fidelity	13 to 19 years old
6	Intimacy versus Isolation	Love	20 to 39 years old
7	Generativity versus Self-Absorption	Care	40 to 64 years old
8	Integrity versus Despair	Wisdom	65 to death

Note. Phipps, A. (2011). Preparing Adolescents for Bariatric Surgery: Foundational Elements Applying Erikson's Theory of Human Development. Retrieved from: dx.doi.org/10.1089/bar.2011.9947. Bariatric Nursing and Surgical Patient Care. Reprinted with permission.

Doctoral students must learn to respond to unfamiliar situations progressing through the doctoral program. Going through the doctoral program, doctoral students strive to increase mental and emotional resources to meet higher standards of graduate academic goals. Adolescents in early stages of life having a higher socio-emotional, state-of-mind have greater academic success because behaviors tend to be low risk (Hurd, Varner, & Rowley, 2013). Positive mentoring relationships have an ability to lead mentees to feel confident about academic tasks and remain focused (Kogan, Brody, & Chen, 2011). The gains mentees have in social-emotional development may lead to better behaviors and mental

attitudes about academic studies (Durlak et al., 2011). Having a positive and confident attitude may assist with doctoral students' ability to complete the doctoral program.

Identity development. It is important for mentors and mentees to have a sense of self-awareness and understand self-identification. To build an effective mentoring relationship, mentors and mentees must understand self-identification, and understand how identity development impacts the mentoring relationship. Each student entering a doctoral program will have different levels of developmental abilities and students may hinder academic growth depending on the level of abilities (Nadelson & Nadelson, 2012). According to education researcher Arthur Chickering, college students must establish a sense of identity to build interpersonal relationship skills (McDowell & Higbee, 2014). Chickering's seven vectors to achieve this goal for college students includes: (a) develop competence, (b) must manage emotions, (c) become more independent, (d) develop interpersonal relationships, (e) establish a sense of identity, (f) create purpose, and (g) developing trustworthiness (McDowell & Higbee, 2014). Identity development is a critical element for doctoral students to develop.

Doctoral students are required to contribute a significant amount of new knowledge to research. Students need to establish not only self-identity, but develop an academic identity while pursuing a doctorate degree (Schulze, 2014). Doctoral students making complex choices and decisions may help students construct the academic identity students are looking for (Ballamingie & Mikeson, 2011). The identity developed amongst doctoral students may help master necessary skills to interact with peers and other scholarly community members that go beyond academic environments (Vekkaila et al., 2012). Confidence and self-awareness was built with students going through this interaction phase. Doctoral students felt this sense of confidence and self-esteem may help them find the doctoral journey much easier to achieve, which may prevent students from dropping out of the program.

Cognitive development. Piaget posited cognitive development as "a progressive reorganization of mental processes resulting in biological maturation and environmental experiences" (McLeod, 2015, para 9) and studied how individuals first learn and start to understand what is learned (Asokan, Surendran, Asokan, & Nuvvula, 2014). The *Encyclopedia of Children's Health* (2015) defines cognitive development as thought process being constructed that includes remembering, solving problems, and making decisions throughout a person's life cycle. A person's cognitive development is important in doctoral mentoring relationships as the competence of the relationship needs to be assessed with each other's cognitive abilities (Lundgren & Orsillo, 2012). The ability to eliminate cognitive dissonance between mentors and mentees is an important element used to match mentors and mentees in the doctoral program.

Theorist Piaget's extensive empirical work and research on cognitive development included acquired complexities of knowledge gained based on the ability to resist any knowledge previously acquired (Borst et al., 2013). The progress of cognitive development was not automatic and involved the interaction of different influences: maturity peek, ongoing active experiences, social interaction, and a progression of emotional balance (Ewing, Foster, & Whittington, 2011). Doctoral mentors had opportunities to influence doctoral mentees' maturity levels, experiences, social interactions, and emotional stability, thus enhancing the mentee's cognitive development.

Retention and success in doctoral education requires cognitive interest to expand inquiry and seek knowledge (Francois, 2014). The learning process is facilitated within and to doctoral students providing a clear, organized, and stable cognitive structure and the ability to process new knowledge. Ifenthaler, Masduki, and Seel (2011) stated unstable and unorganized cognitive structures can inhibit the ability to retain knowledge and the learning process. Doctoral mentors have an ability to assist mentees to increase cognitive development by role-modeling maturity, sharing experiences, and providing emotional stability. Advanced cognitive development initiated seeking and applying new knowledge for dissertation research.

Conflicting Theories

Academic researchers have provided different theories on establishing effective mentor/mentee relationships. Business and academic leaders used different theories when building a mentoring program. Mentoring programs were formulated through theoretical structures that helped businesses and academic institutions determine the concept and implementation of mentoring (Dominguez & Hager, 2013). According to Fletcher and Mullen (2012), inconsistencies existed in mentor/mentee theories as mentoring programs across academia tried to evaluate and create effective mentoring programs.

Levinson et al. (1978) posited a traditional mentoring relationship theory of mentors which was viewed as self-developed. Self-developed younger mentors have been effective compared to older mentors because school connectedness is promoted (Smith & Holloman, 2013). Younger mentors felt more connected to doctoral students because younger mentors experienced 'being' a student mentee more recently than older mentors. A downside for doctoral students having a younger mentor is the experience level of the younger mentors. Older mentors naturally serve as mentors and provide a considerable amount to doctoral students' cognitive and social development (Smith & Holloman, 2013).

In contrast, Kram's (1985) mentoring relationship theory proposed mentees could receive support from multiple mentors, which is identified as developmental networks (Mundia & Iravo, 2014). Developmental networks may involve multiple people that share information and provide mentoring support to doctoral students (Lunsford, 2014). Developmental networks benefited doctoral students because the network provides career and psychosocial support (Wendy & Kram, 2010). Developmental networks could be instrumental in developing doctoral students' confidence to complete doctoral programs while building healthy mentoring relationships.

Kram (1983) developed four stages of a mentoring relationship cycle: initiation, cultivation, separation, and redefinition. In the initiation phase, expectations are clarified between mentors and mentees in the mentoring relationship. Mentees begin learning from mentors in the cultivation phase whereas the separation phase mentees begin working independently and demonstrating confidence in learning skills (Kram, 1983).

The last stage, redefinition, is one in which the mentoring relationship was terminated and became mutually supportive (Kram, 1985). The progression of the mentor / mentee relationship, defined by Kram's four mentoring stages, has been embraced by researchers, yet also had recognized the length of each cycle may vary considerably.

The length of time between each phase seemed to be unclear when moving from one stage to the next in Kram's mentoring cycle (Chao, 1997; Pollock, 1995). Kram's phases of the mentoring cycle was intended for traditional mentoring consisting of one-to-one and face-to-face mentoring styles. According to Scandura and Pellegrini (2007), Kram's phases did not seem to apply to other mentoring concepts that included peer mentoring, protégés having more than one mentor, and mentoring through new technology. Passmore, Peterson, and Freire (2013) noted theorists consider some mentoring relationships to be long-term, while others may not be as supportive, thus considered short-lived.

Traditional mentoring has met with other conflicting theories pertaining to relational mentoring. According to Levinson et al. (1978), traditional mentoring focuses on self and one-directional learning. The theory behind Levinson et al. (1978) may work well when the focus is primarily on instruction, but two directional mentoring also captures the full dynamics of the mentoring relationship. Two directional mentoring has been found to be successful because the mentors and mentees learn and grow through the relationship experience (Jordan, 2103). Another traditional mentoring theory is the mode of influence is set on hierarchical levels (Santora, Mason, & Sheahan, 2013). The relational growth occurs with the bond and connection built between mentors and mentees (Jordan, 2013).

Mentors at a Glance

Students pursuing doctorate degrees need guidance through the academic journey. To ensure doctoral students successfully complete doctoral programs, students are paired with mentors for support and guidance. The role mentors play in doctoral students' journeys help students reach goals and assist students working to full potential (Lundgren & Orsillo, 2012). Mentors providing different levels of support may help in the dissertation process and influences productivity output amongst faculty (Ugrin, Odom, Pearson, & Bahmanziari, 2012). The role of mentor can be overlooked, yet is important for academic institutions to pay attention to mentoring programs (Gutiérrez, 2012).

Doctoral students should be committed to academic work, while mentors should be committed to providing the best service for mentees. To effectively achieve a good mentor and mentee relationship, a time commitment must be established by mentors. Mentors may run into obstacles at times, which could prohibit the necessary time needed between mentors and mentees (Singh & Mahomed, 2013). Mentors might be discouraged from mentoring students because of the time commitment involved (Reddick, 2012). In the long-run, sufficient time should be allotted for mentors to effectively build the mentoring relationship (Singh & Mahomed, 2013).

Mentors build a relationship with protégés by guiding and transferring knowledge and skills for the protégé to duplicate that process when protégés become mentors (Brondyk & Searby, 2013). Mentors must demonstrate effective mentoring skills to accomplish the task of passing on mentoring skills to mentees. Effective mentoring can be evaluated by instant feedback promoted through the mentor's efforts (Kiran et al., 2012). Mentors gaining instant feedback may help mentors recognize deficiencies and help promote better mentoring (Kiran et al., 2012). Understanding and correcting mentoring deficiencies helps to establish an effective mentoring relationship.

Mentor Relationship Building

A mentoring relationship has been defined as a relationship developed on a sponsored level where a person more experienced and a person less experienced are paired together for knowledge sharing with a goal of progressing the mentee to the next level (Noe, 1988). Mentoring relationships are developed with the type of assistance provided by mentors (Kram, 1985; Scandura & Ragins, 1993). The mentoring functions provided by mentors include: (a) career support, (b) psychosocial support, and (c) role modeling (Chun, Sosik, & Yun, 2012). For mentor relationships to be effective, both mentor and mentee have roles to play and obligations to fulfill.

Mentors provide experience and skills and the mentee provides a personal set of skills and experiences to the relationship (Evans & Forbes, 2012). Doctoral students know how to achieve goals, but mentors must get acquainted with mentees to ensure the identified goals are attainable and achieved (Evans & Forbes, 2012). To achieve the goals, a mutual understanding between mentors and mentees must exist on the different types of formal and informal relationships necessary to succeed (Anastasia, Skinner, & Mundhenk, 2012). To help clarify mentoring relationship goals, mentors and mentees must understand the relationships connection and purpose (Anastasia et al., 2012).

Informal mentoring is something not structurally set up between mentors and mentees. The relationships built from informal mentoring are done instinctively with no outside help from academic institutions (Laiho & Brandt, 2012). Mentors and mentees feel mutual connections, which may potentially form into a mentoring relationship (Elizabeth et al., 2012). Relationships developed though informal mentoring can happen by chance, and though this type of mentoring can last a long time, it takes time to develop (Haggard, 2012). Lack of organized effort can be a challenge developing informal mentoring relationships. The relationship has the potential to lack integrity of allowing for professional feedback for mentors and mentees, which causes problems for students' doctoral journey (Reinstein, Sinason, & Fogarty, 2012).

Doctoral students face different challenges working towards a doctoral degree, and academic leaders assist students in establishing formal mentoring programs (Laiho & Brandt, 2012). Doctoral students presented with formal mentoring are offered an advantage over informal mentoring for doctoral students and helps students comprehend institutional structure and its framework (Metzger et al., 2013). Formal mentoring is a little different from informal mentoring in the way it is structured. To distinguish between the two, developing a formal mentor relationship is formed in a structured environment where there is an outside influence or third-party, personnel pairing mentors and mentees together (Joo, Sushko, & McLean, 2012). Challenges arise with formal mentoring when formal mentoring programs fail to align with how informal mentoring relationships are developed (Cornelius & Wood, 2012). Doctoral students may feel forced to accept a mentor, which could lead to resentment and failure for the student to complete doctoral programs.

Compatibility

Academic institutions developed mentoring programs by assisting mentors and mentees in understanding mentoring relationships and help develop a compatible relationship (Poronsky, 2012). Compatible mentors and mentees set realistic goals and pay close attention to relationships that may promote competence, productivity, and professional growth (Poronsky, 2012). It is important for academic institutions to match mentors with doctoral students who share similar personal qualities for mentoring relationships to work (Wang & Fulton, 2012). According to Akanni (2011), mentees dealt with negative experiences when poorly matched with an incompatible mentor. Mentoring relationships should begin with mentors and students having a common goal and sharing similar interest (Sanfey, Hollands, & Gantt, 2013).

Ineffective relationships developed between mentors and mentees take place when the social skills of each member are incompatible. Ineffective relationships can come from either member, but socially skilled mentees are usually matched with mentors displaying poor social skills (Wu et al., 2012). Mentors are faced with displaying these types of poor social skills because mentors adjudicate the type and how much mentoring is provided (Wu et al., 2012). Incompatible issues can be minimized when mentors and mentees have similar thinking styles, thus maximizing the efficiency of the mentoring relationship (Terry, DeMichiell, & Williams, 2009).

Time Investment

Building effective mentoring relationships is critical for mentors and mentees; it takes time to build a relationship. Mentors oversee the protégé's project ensuring everything is being followed according to policy and gives the protégé advice and support (St-jean & Audet, 2012). Mentors are also seen as a parent (figure), investing the same amount of time, emotional resources, and energy to ensure mentees are doing everything needed to complete projects (Sanfey et al., 2013). Mentees rely on mentors for moral support when needed, which adds mentors' responsibilities.

Doctoral students need experienced mentors that will invest time, commitment, and efforts developing student's personal and professional growth (Rekha & Ganesh, 2012). A mentor's personal commitment to mentees is time-intensive, yet crucial for doctoral student's success in degree completion (Hagemeier, Murawski, & Popovich, 2013). Formal training for mentors should be adequate to meet the needs of mentees because time commitment to relationship development is critical (Anastasia et al., 2012). Mentoring programs at academic institutions help mentors develop effective relationships through formal training (Barnetz & Feigin, 2012). Mentors getting the most out of formal training help produce effective mentoring relationships.

Academic institutions place mentoring high on its priority list and regard it as an important aspect for doctoral students' development. Adequate time should be provided for mentors ensuring mentees get the attention deserved. Challenges arise when there is a lack of time for mentors to assist mentees on doctoral journeys (Singh & Mahomed, 2013). Additional time should be given to mentors to assist mentees, still allowing mentors to stay on track of personal workload commitments (Singh & Mahomed, 2013). Time is an important component for doctoral students and mentors; providing insufficient time to complete tasking and mutual responsibilities can hinder mentoring relationships.

Lack of Support

Students pursuing doctorate degrees face challenges and obstacles. For doctoral students to overcome these barriers, a support system needs to be in place to get through those difficult times. Mentees have expectations that mentors will provide guidance and support (Kram, 1983). One type of support doctoral students need is psychological support, which makes students feel more comfortable by addressing emotional and personal needs, and providing moral support to balance out the student's academic demands (Ligadu, 2012).

Support levels needed by each doctoral student will vary for each student. Mentoring support is developed to meet each student's needs and to receive individualized feedback from mentors (Utrilla & Grande, 2012). Mentoring practices, at times, can be difficult because of complex structures in the mentoring processes (Brondyk & Searby, 2013). Incorporating the processes of an effective mentoring partnership takes time and effort to ensure mentors and mentees receive sufficient support (Sarri, 2011). Mentors and mentees need to communicate personal needs to one another to make sure there is mutually beneficial understanding.

Mentors at academic institutions have multiple responsibilities that could have negative effects on mentees. High-workload demands, employee shortages, and lack of time management practices could result in mentors ineffectively managing their assigned mentees (Morton, 2013). With the mentorship workload, academic institutions could have mentoring programs where mentors are assigned a limited number of mentees. The number of mentees assigned to a mentor can be overwhelming, which can be stressful for the mentoring relationship; resulting in potential jeopardy for the mentees' needs (Lundgren & Orsillo, 2012). Mentors ae over mentee capacity find it to be an over-commitment to their own time availability.

Unclear Expectations

Clear expectations in developing mentoring relationships are critical for scholars and mentors. Doctoral students and mentors will have a series of expectations on minimum requirements or expectations from each other. Mutual expectations may be addressed in a variety of ways to fit the needs of students and mentors. Expectations can be concrete or generic, self directed or participative, and could be vocalized or assumed (Huskins et al., 2011). Once expectations were clearly defined, academic leaders were ready to guide mentees through the doctoral process (Evans & Laura, 2012).

Unclear expectations can lead to challenges for students pursuing doctoral degrees. Academic institutions should develop mentoring policies in the best interest of mentors and mentees by developing clear expectations (Anastasia et al., 2012). Mentors need to lead when communicating expectations in the mentoring relationship (Barratt-Pugh, 2012). When mentors were not capable of taking the lead, there could be potential of disappointing mentees by failing to meet mentees' needs and expectations (Hamlin & Sage, 2011). Expectations should be made clear, concise, and agreed upon by both the mentor and mentee.

Trust

One of the most important components to a mentoring relationship is building trust between mentors and mentees. Mentors are taught how to build trust and rapport, which are positive characteristics helping mentees reach goals (Rekha & Ganesh, 2012). To overcome difficult issues between mentors and mentees, building a high level of trust is essential in meeting the demands of getting things done (Cowin, Cohen, Ciechanowski, & Orozco, 2012). Mentoring functions provided by mentors to mentees may build effective relationships and assist in building a trusting one (Wu et al., 2012). Lines of communication need to be open and a mutual respect needs to be established for mentors and mentees.

Challenges arise when there is a communication breakdown or lack of, which impacts the mentoring relationship (Leck, Elliott, & Rockwell, 2012). Communication is important and it can have either a negative or positive effect on the mentoring relationship's levels of trust (Fischer, 2013). Honesty is another essential component to building a trusting mentoring relationship. Relationships could be hindered because of uncertainty of honesty; to have an effective relationship, honesty must be included (Sanfey et al., 2013). Having a trusting mentoring relationship helped build the mentees' confidence level to complete doctoral programs.

Building a mentoring relationship is not easy; the trust that goes into mentor relationships may not happen immediately. Trust is built on emotional levels when mentees unmask vulnerabilities to perspective mentors, hoping they will not be taken advantage of because of the mentee's exposure of those vulnerabilities (Hills, 2013). A trustworthy relationship between mentors and mentees should be developed to create a mutual learning experience and enhance development of mentoring programs (Vaughns, 2013). Without trust, mentoring relationships become uneasy and mentors or mentees can feel insecure and uncomfortable. An effective mentoring relationship depends on a mutually-trusting relationship.

Interpersonal Relationship

Mentors and mentees offer different personal characteristics when forming a mentoring relationship. Differences in each participant's characteristics will affect the development of the relationship (Huang & Weng, 2012).

Interpersonal attraction is an important factor when mentees are searching for mentors (Huang & Weng, 2012). It is this interpersonal comfort level for mentees that allow mentors and mentees to communicate effectively. Doctoral students and mentors experience an effective relationship when there is a high degree of interpersonal comfort (Yim & Waters, 2013). Mentors should demonstrate a balance of power and influence over mentees. Comfort levels need to be established by mentors and mentees while effective communication is developed between both parties, which helps the mentoring relationship process (Rusbult, Martz, & Agnew, 1998). Mentoring relationships may create a safe haven for mentors and mentees through a psychologically-based interpersonal support (Ortiz-Walters & Gilson, 2005).

One way to measure interpersonal relationships with compatibility levels between mentors and mentees is by using a Leader Member Exchange (LMX) measurement tool. LMX is used in the mentoring relationship process measuring the social exchange quality in the relationship. The LMX measurement tool measures the social exchange between mentors and mentees. Doctoral students that have low stress in the mentoring relationship are associated with high Leader Mix Exchange (LMX; Ugrin, Odom, & Pearson, 2008). Doctoral students associated with high LMX may be more successful completing doctoral programs because of minimized stress resulting from a mutually compatible mentoring relationship.

Distance versus Traditional Doctoral Learning and Mentoring

Establishing an effective mentoring relationship is important for doctoral students regardless of school setting (physical or virtual). Whether it is the traditional face-to-face environment or an online environment, the mentoring relationship should be beneficial for mentors and mentees. Doctoral students are lacking a clear vision, at times, for specific and strategic goals and may be unsure how to use mentors to get mentor relationship benefits (McKeage, Tischler, & Biberman, 2013). Mentoring programs should have its largest emphasis on doctoral students being guided through the completion of doctoral programs (Horowitz & Christopher, 2013). Horowitz and Christopher (2013) state mentors should not only guide doctoral students to program completion, but should teach and/or model to students how to become mentors as well.

Technology

Technological advances are continuing to change, and these changes dictate how various businesses operate. Technological changes taking place are becoming the norm and being accepted as one of the most essential elements on methods to improve economic growth (Stadler, 2012). Academic institutions are changing the way education is delivered as the number of online course offerings is increasing (Lloyd, Byrne, & McCoy, 2012). Face-to-face enrollment for academic institutions are declining (Allen & Seaman, 2013) and enrollment for online (virtual classes) education has continued to climb (Martin, 2013). As online education continued to increase in demand, academic institutions must expand how courses are delivered to keep current students and attract new ones (Gray, 2013). No matter what delivery style of education doctoral students seek, academic institutions must be consistent in developing an effective mentoring program.

Distance Learning

The way education is delivered to college students today is different from how education was delivered in the past. Over the past few years, distance learning has experienced an explosive climb and continues to grow annually (Bolliger & Halupa, 2012). Academic technology innovators have allowed college students to attend classes at home without stepping foot inside a classroom. Responsibilities students face today have changed, which makes students opt to get education via online environments (Hrastinski & Jaldemark, 2012). To lower educational expenses, many students are choosing this alternative instead of living on campus where various brick and mortar schools may cost more than attending online classes (Bolliger & Halupa, 2012).

Mentoring students who are attending an online program is relatively new as doctoral programs at different academic institutions are establishing and facilitating more online (virtual) courses. These academic institutions set up mentoring programs that vary depending on the school's structure and available resources to establish the program (Guise & Fink, 2013). Mentoring relationships established between mentors and students should be similar – as if the student attended face-to-face classes and mentees are able to physically meet with their mentor. Mentors and mentees must be in sync; communication is important for doctoral students attending an online program. An effective mentoring relationship needs to be built between mentors and doctoral students and cannot take place without proper communication (Brannagan & Oriol, 2014).

Mentoring has taken on new boundaries with technology advancements that go beyond the traditional, in-person relationship mentors have with mentees (Poronsky, 2012). Being able to mentor doctoral students through virtual means provides a more or increased flexible environment where meetings do not need to be face-to-face, but can be done via technological means such as e-mail, telephone, and texting (Poronsky, 2012).

College students feel the need to have things instantly, and the use of technology helps ensure faster decisions and communications with faculty members (Evans & Forbes, 2012). Academic institutions must ensure students' needs are met for the mentoring relationship to work. Academic leaders responsible for mentoring programs may invest time and effort to create a structure where developmental relationships are going to succeed in an online environment (Shojai, Davis, & Root, 2014).

Doctoral students attending online classes may find different advantages pertaining to the mentoring process. One of the major advantages of having a virtual mentor is the instant access the students have, and the ability to instantly interact with the mentor through different technologies available, such as chat rooms (Knouse, 2013). Virtual interactions challenges mentors to have a closer relationship with mentees. Collaborative interaction ensures mentee's concerns are addressed, which establishes a better connection between mentors and mentees (Starr-Glass, 2013). Another advantage to virtual mentoring – mentees 'open up' more without having the feeling of being evaluated, which can be implied from face-to-face mentoring (Delaney, 2012).

Development of new technology played an important role in the development of mentoring programs at academic institutions. Doctoral students have a variety of ways to communicate with mentors while attending online classes. These communications can consist of social networks, e-mail, instant messaging, text messaging, and video conferencing, which can develop a relationship independent of geographical barriers (Butler, Whiteman, & Crow, 2013). By having means of communication such as video conferencing, the connectedness between mentors and mentees was met through these levels of technology (Cynthia et al., 2012). Interpersonal connections developed helps in obtaining an effective mentoring relationship that would correlate with a face-to- face mentoring relationship.

Traditional Learning

Technology has changed the way many organizations and businesses do business. Increases of technological advances are forcing academic institutions to incorporate new and existing, but unused electronic technology to keep up with academic changes (Michael, 2012). Changes being implemented may affect mentoring programs as more academic institutions are delivering doctoral programs online. Mentoring doctoral students will become more virtual than face-to-face but this may also create new barriers. Doctoral students may find that doing research in an online environment is challenging because there is no direct support from academic administrators (Ewing et al., 2012). According to Ewing et al., (2012) doctoral students' feeling of insufficient support needs to be addressed to build an effective mentoring relationship.

Academic administrators have been challenged on what constitutes an effective mentoring relationship between mentors and mentees (Yob & Crawford, 2012). Students receiving virtual mentoring may help doctoral students express more on difficult matters that could not be handled if it were face-to-face (Iacovelli & Johnson, 2012). Luxuries of having the option to interact virtually also come with challenges where there is a lack of access for students and an unstable infrastructure (Ware & Ramos, 2013). Virtual mentoring could provide an impersonal feeling because of the non-existence of the face-to-face interaction between mentors and mentees (Poronsky, 2012). Exchanges of information are transmitted in the form of only words and messages received from mentors or mentees could be incorrectly interpreted or perceived (Poronsky, 2012). Although the use of virtual mentoring can be considered the preferred method for some doctoral students, having a face-to-face interaction may improve the mentoring relationship (Meyer & Warren-Gordon, 2013).

Students interested in earning a doctorate degree must have a support system in place to ensure the successful completion of the doctoral program. Some of the issues important to note for new students were doctoral student's attrition rates and the time it takes to complete the doctoral degree (Maldonado, Wiggers, & Arnold, 2013). Having an optimal mentoring program to cover these issues is important to help doctoral students succeed (Nakanjako et al., 2014). Another essential element for successful completion is effective communication, because it influenced the mentoring relationship between mentors and mentees (Yim & Waters, 2013). Mentors and mentees that established effective communication in the mentoring relationship may have a better understanding of specific information (Yim & Waters, 2013). Whether a doctoral student is attending an on-campus, traditional school or taking doctoral studies online, having an effective mentoring relationship is important to successfully complete the doctoral program.

Negative and Positive Impact on Mentoring Relationships

Academic achievement is one of the most important educational resources in our nation, and constant initiatives are developed to increase this effort (Gordon, Downey, & Bangert, 2013). Academic institutions are also focusing on initiatives that help retain doctoral students and assist in completing doctorate degrees (Di Pierro, 2012). While increasing these efforts, doctoral students embark on a journey to further educational goals, but are usually unprepared for the level of work required and need assistance in meeting these goals (Opayemi, 2012). Assistance comes in the form of mentoring and building a mentoring relationship between a mentor and a doctoral student. Goals of the mentoring process at academic institutions are to develop the student's personal and academic skills to successfully complete the doctoral program (Holley & Caldwell, 2012). By establishing and understanding the different types of mentoring relationships to complete doctorate degrees, it is necessary to develop a consistent set of positive outcomes to prevent negative ones (Anastasia et al., 2012). Both the mentor and protégé should understand there can be both negative or positive outcomes from the mentoring relationship.

Negative Impact

Attrition. Pursuing a doctorate degree is a major step for those that want to receive a career-based, terminal graduate degree. Completing the doctoral degree is not an easy task, and academic institutions need to have a system to guide students through the process to prevent students from dropping out of the doctoral program. Academic institutions are cognizant of the retention of doctoral students, which hovers around a nation-wide attrition rate of 50% (Di Pierro, 2012). Because of this high attrition rate, it is implied school administrators must implement a process to attract and retain doctoral students to reverse this trend (Ampaw & Jaeger, 2012; Di Pierro, 2012). Mentoring relationships should be part of the retention process as this relationship provides a support level that goes beyond the typical advising relationship for a specific course from another faculty (Holley & Caldwell, 2012).

Different elements and components play a part in doctoral students dropping from the doctoral program. Program drop outs can be personal or financially-based issues, but it could also be associated with unsuccessful mentoring relationships. Experiences doctoral student's encounter in the mentoring process has an impact on the student's retention or attrition (Maher & Macallister, 2013). Academic cultures established by administrators for doctoral programs affect student dropout, and mentors contribute to that environment (Cassuto, 2013). If there is a negative relationship established between doctoral students and the mentors, students have the potential of exiting the program or the school before completion (O'Keeffe, 2013).

Under-Achieving. Building a positive mentoring relationship is one of the most important things doctoral students will face while pursuing a doctoral degree. Doctoral students should feel comfortable in the relationship because the mentoring relationship is a critical aspect to personal growth and development (Sanfey et al., 2013). Positive relationships built between mentors and students help students complete doctoral programs. Communication is crucial and often a barrier in a relationship preventing students from reaching academic goals (Ligadu, 2012). The primary goal for each doctoral student is successfully completing the doctoral degree.

Mentors should be experienced in effectively communicating with mentees for a positive academic experience. Negative outcomes doctoral students face come from not being well informed and having unclear direction from mentors, which include expectations and the doctoral degree process (Barnes & Randall, 2012). If mentors lack the ability to communicate effectively, the academic institution should implement a training program to assist mentors in communicating the obligations between both parties (Haggard, 2012). Not being proactive may have resulted in doctoral students not achieving academic goals.

Stress. Processes of pursuing a doctorate degree requires hard work, dedication, and intense preparation (Black, 2012). Doctoral students face pressures of completing academics goals, as well as personal and professional involvement with school faculty. Academic institutions should provide a positive learning experience for each student and to identify and prevent any stressors inhibiting students from progressing (Madhan, Ojha, & Gayathri, 2011). Stressful emotions doctoral students felt may have come from perceptions of neglect from mentors or school administrators (Veal, Bull, & Miller, 2012). Emotional support mentors provide was important in helping doctoral students cope with stress, and with an unsupportive mentor, graduate students may have been prone to quitting (Rigg, Day, & Adler, 2013)

Positive Impact

School performance. Doctoral students are faced with different challenges in a doctoral program. A one-on-one mentor/student relationship may be enhanced by being paired with an effective mentor (Pryce, 2012). A mentor/student relationship is established to help guide students to perform effectively to complete the doctoral program. Mentors that possess effective mentoring skills enable doctoral students to work independently and give students the confidence to perform independent research (Petersen, Eggert, Grümmer, Schara, & Sauerwein, 2012). Mentors could empower doctoral students into performing at a level consistent with the institutions' norms (Sugimoto, 2012b).

A doctoral student's performance in school is important with trying to balance academic life with personal life. Doctoral students' success with research projects depends on the relationship developed between mentors and mentees (Ezebilo, 2012). Benefits of effective mentoring included improvement in the doctoral student's school performance, which furthered academic and professional success (Rueywei, Shih-Ying, & Shin-Lung, 2011). Increasing the focus on mentoring programs at academic institutions is considered an advantage on the mentoring process (Gordon et al., 2013). Relationships established between mentors and mentees should correlate with the doctoral student's success.

Interpersonal competence. People who pursue doctoral degrees are making a decision that requires patience, time, and effort. An essential element to school success was the doctoral student's ability to be engaged (Hafen et al., 2012). Social differences that existed between mentors and mentees should not be set aside for students to achieve academic goals (George & Sebastian, 2012). Mentors should relinquish control to doctoral student's academic learning; doctoral students need to take control of how they learn (Yob & Crawford, 2012) and mentors that are too controlling may hinder the doctoral student's ability to grow, because mentees were still co-dependent.

Doctoral students who successfully complete a doctoral degree have dealt with people from different social levels. Students enter doctoral programs with the expectation of succeeding with the help of mentors, while experiencing personal growth through social interactions (Callary, Werthner, & Trudel, 2012). Interpersonal competence established between mentors and mentees was a direct reflection of how mentors guided mentees through the doctoral process. Doctoral students and mentors who experienced a high level of interpersonal competence in the mentoring relationship will have a positive effect on students; that social comfort facilitated a stronger understanding of the doctoral process (Yim & Waters, 2013). Understanding the doctoral process helped doctoral students to be confident and independent when socializing with others.

Mental attitude. Processes of earning a doctoral degree can be stressful for students who cannot handle additional life-situation pressures to achieve a higher level of education. The complexity of the doctoral process can have a negative effect on potential students; a factor that contributes to the student's success is the mentoring relationship (Doloriert, Sambrook, & Stewart, 2012). An essential criterion for establishing the mentoring relationship is mentors providing emotional support to the mentees.

According to past research, mentors who were effective attended to mentees emotional and their pedagogical needs (Gilles, Carrillo, Wang, Stegall, & Bumgarner, 2013). Emotional support provided by mentors went beyond academic support, because psychosocial support produced a high level of satisfaction between mentors and mentees (Eby et al., 2013). Mentors who provided a mixture of academic and emotional support helped doctoral students progress and enhanced personal growth (Yob & Crawford, 2012).

Mentor Characteristics

Admission to any doctoral program is an achievement for any student. Once in the doctoral program, students must be guided by mentors during each step of the doctoral program. Mentors should possess certain characteristics in mentoring styles to help doctoral students reach academic goals. A characteristic each mentor possesses is perceived, by doctoral students, as important traits for successful completion of doctoral programs (Houser, Lemmons, & Cahill, 2013). The following mentoring characteristics were described to show the importance of mentors possessing characteristics guiding doctoral students throughout the mentoring relationship:

Experience

Mentors should be well-equipped to assist doctoral students with successfully completing academic goals. Different characteristics are associated with effective mentors, and one of these consists of having a high degree of experience over mentees (Kiersma et al., 2012). Mentors paired with doctoral students provided advice, guidance, and support through personal and professional experiences (Yob & Crawford, 2012). Not only should mentors possess the necessary experience, but should also be qualified to be mentors for doctoral students (Aslan & Öcal, 2012). Mentors' credentials can help students feel more comfortable when working with mentees on research projects.

Leadership

Many titles are associated with the term mentor and include coach, teacher, and advisor, but most importantly – leader (Healy, Cantillon, Malone, & Kerin, 2012). Leadership is about transformation, ability to make changes, and help people progress (Howard & Hirani, 2013). Mentors were in position to help others move forward by encouraging growth and development as leaders (Jor'dan, Muñoz, Figlar, & Rust, 2013). Mentors used leadership skills as a gift to encourage and inspire mentees (Laughlin & Moore, 2012). Mentors that possessed valued leadership skills helped develop mentees' self-awareness, and through the mentor-mentee relationship, mentees could turn into leaders (Jor'dan et al., 2013). Students successfully completing doctoral programs were guided by a combination of traits mentors possessed.

Communication

Building a mentoring relationship between mentors and mentees can have challenges, but effective communication could eliminate those challenges. According to Buzatu and Pipas (2014) "the ability to communicate is an essential mechanism in the construction and development of interpersonal human relationships, to achieve social integration" (p. 681). Mentors and mentees needed to know and understand each other on different levels to expand communication efforts (Sabie & Androniceanu, 2012). Mentors and mentees must communicate expectations and goals needed to be reached to maintain an effective relationship (Ricks, 2013). Mentors' communication skills could influence the mentoring process, and the outstanding quality mentors have may better supported mentees (Yim & Waters, 2013). Ineffective mentor-mentee relationships may be due to poor communication (Brooks, 2012), therefore effective mentoring relationships may depend on highly skilled communication practices between mentor and mentee.

Self-Efficacy

A mentor's self-efficacy and the level mentees sought support from mentors could affect the mentoring relationship (Karcher, Nakkula, & Harris, 2005). Human behavior is stimulated in a variety of ways, and one-way that self-influence greatly stimulated behavior was by self-efficacy (Bandura, 1986). Self-efficacy dealt with peoples' beliefs in the ability to complete a goal or task (Bandura, 1986). Developing a mentoring relationship set the stage for mentors and mentees to work together effectively by allowing the opportunity to understand each other's interests, beliefs, and goals (Wang et al., 2010). Mentors built trust, which motivated proactivity in mentees' activities. Being proactive in the mentees life developed mentees self-efficacy (Wang et al., 2010).

Self-efficacy beliefs could potentially affect actions, motivation, and emotions and may be important in pursuing goals (Lightsey, 1999). Bandura (1986) stated people are proactive and determined to accomplish goals, and self-reflecting; similar to how architects painted personal pictures of the future. Because people shaped the environment and their surroundings, self-efficacy beliefs are instrumental on how people's physical and social environments were painted (Lightsey, 1999). The paintings of self-efficacy aligned with mentees' development during the doctoral program and successfully having completed the doctoral program.

Motivation

Levels of motivation were exhibited in individuals in all aspects of life. The different levels depend on the individual and what priorities were established for individuals (Hegarty & Del Vecchio, 2012). Mentors paired with doctoral students were selected to establish an effective relationship and helped student's complete dissertations and graduate, yet mentors must be motivated to take on the job of mentoring doctoral students (Straus & Sackett, 2012). Mentors should evaluate levels of motivation to provide the best support and guidance possible to protégés (DeMoss, Clem, & Wilson, 2012). Mentees should be engaged by mentors offering different opportunities to benefit in building a relationship (Keller & Pryce, 2012). One of the greatest feelings and rewards for mentors and mentees was establishing an effective mentoring relationship comfortable to both parties (Ricks, 2013).

Emotional Intelligence

Mentoring is not an easy process and can have effects on the emotional state of mentors. Emotions play a role in everyday lives and directs human behavior in a variety of ways (Joshith, 2012). Mentoring doctoral students could be an emotional process when dealing with a diverse group of students; mentors should understand how to handle situations by understanding the concept of emotional intelligence.

According to Schutte, Malouff, and Thorsteinsson (2013), "emotional intelligence consists of adaptive emotional functioning involving inter-related competencies relating to perception, understanding, utilizing and managing emotions in the self and others" (p. 56). Mentors should have the ability to recognize the emotions of doctoral students in any situation and relieve perceived stresses to enhance the students' emotional well-being (McCallum, 2013). Part of being an effective mentor is recognizing the emotional state of mentees (Laughlin & Moore, 2012). The emotional support mentors provided to mentees strengthened the mentoring relationship.

Moral Composition

Mentors are considered as leaders to mentees and the moral composition should be flawless when establishing a mentoring relationship. Since mentors are considered leaders, leadership characteristics such as integrity, character, and being trustworthy should be encompassed (Gaiter, 2013). Confidentiality in the mentoring relationship must be established to keep the mentor's integrity from being jeopardized (Aslan & Öcal, 2012). Mentors may find one attribute mentees are trying to learn or emulate is personal integrity (Belachew, 2012). Mentors must also communicate how important ethics are when building a mentoring relationship and working on the research project (Culp & Urtel, 2013).

Mutual trust is a moral composition that should be developed in the mentoring relationship. A key mentorship attribute was in having the ability to build trust between the mentor-mentee (Rekha & Ganesh, 2012). Building trust is essential in the initial phase of building the mentoring relationship (Shahid & Azhar, 2013). When mentors were unable to establish and build a foundation of trust, the relationship may have failed as a result (Krause-Parello, Sarcone, Samms, & Boyd, 2013).

Reputation

Mentors are perceived to have more knowledge and experience over protégés. Just as mentors should have more of an experience level over protégés, mentors should also have a good reputation of being an effective mentor. Doctoral students understand the importance of mentors was in having an approved reputation (Zinko, Gentry, Hall, & Grant, 2012). Mentors should have a good reputation of having provided outstanding service to mentees and being readily available when needed by mentees (Sanfey et al., 2013). Another reputation mentors are measured against is academic success – how others saw mentors – both personally and professionally (Straus & Sackett, 2012). Mentors should also have a reputation of eagerness to learn while mentoring others. Not only should mentees be evaluated on performance, but mentors should seek evaluation from mentees on the mentor's performance level (Straus & Sackett, 2012). The evaluation process was where mentors may make changes in the mentoring approach.

Cultural Influences

Culture in which mentors and mentees are accustomed includes beliefs, values, and concepts inherited from surroundings throughout life (Tagreed, 2012). Culture can be visible things, including the clothes people wear or an individual's religious beliefs; the invisible aspects of culture pertains to what an individual has nurtured within (Kent et al.,

2013). Different cultural backgrounds can hinder the mentoring relationships effectiveness because of differing beliefs. Conflict can also arise because of generational cultural differences and age gaps between mentors and mentees leaving a misunderstanding in the developing relationship (Merriweather & Morgan, 2013).

School administration and leadership must make it a priority to respect cultural differences and respond appropriately to the differences between students and faculty (Lofthouse & Wright, 2012). Academic institutions must find ways to incorporate support for cultural diversity in mentoring relationships (Brondyk & Searby, 2013). Cultural differences addressed and built into a mentoring program can impact a student's retention or degree completion (Di Pierro, 2012). Developing new identities for mentors and mentees are formed from differences in cultural backgrounds (Lofthouse & Wright, 2012). New identities will establish the expectations between mentors and mentees, and define the cultural values of academic institutions (Lofthouse & Wright, 2012).

Mentoring Programs

Academic institutions incorporate mentoring programs for doctoral students to help facilitate effective matching to mentors. Mentoring programs established at academic institutions can also be referred to as school-based mentoring programs forming mentoring relationships between mentors and mentees (Gordon et al., 2013). Support must come from senior leadership for the mentoring program to be successful. A clear understanding of what the programs' objectives are and how it will be measured are essential (Kiran et al., 2012). Another aspect to building a successful mentoring program is having a mentor training system defining mentor roles, processes, and procedures (Kiran et al., 2012). Mentorship training is an effective resource to help develop effective mentoring relationships.

Mentoring programs are implemented to produce positive outcomes pertaining to building a mentoring relationship. Developing a mentoring program takes time and can be difficult due to the complex nature of its processes and procedures (Brondyk & Searby, 2013). The complex nature correlates to various meaning of what mentoring is, and that has an impact on its conception (Brondyk & Searby, 2013). By building an effective mentoring relationship, doctoral students build up confidence in doing research and have a better chance to successfully complete the dissertation (Kiersma et al., 2012).

Relevant Studies

Several relevant studies have been conducted on the attrition rate of doctoral students and the impact it has on mentoring relationships. Williams (2012) explored the phenomena of doctoral students and wanted to seek a determination as to why some doctoral students finish doctoral degrees and some do not. Williams' (2012) phenomenological study of 11 doctoral students at Eagle University showed several factors were related to doctoral students not completing the doctoral program. One issue students dealt with was a shift in their own personal goals. Setting realistic goals is a major component to earning a doctoral degree (Smith & Delmore, 2007). Williams (2012) stated that psychological issues were reasons doctoral students quit seemingly or are correlated with inaccurate expectations of the doctoral educational journey. One area the study identified as having a significant impact on completion and attrition was the mentoring relationship between the mentor and mentee (Williams, 2012). Financial status also played a part with students dropping out. Students who spent their own money instead of using other financial resources were prone to drop out after their own finances were exhausted.

Another study, related to attrition rates in doctoral programs, was conducted by Wyman (2012). Wyman's (2012) hermeneutic[1] phenomenological study of 10 participants having lived experiences with enrollment in online Doctor of Education programs across the United States showed dropouts in doctoral programs were due to shifts in life experiences. Breaking enrollment involved doctoral students who withdrew from the doctoral program. The purpose of Wyman's (2012) study was to explore strategies for reducing attrition of doctoral students. Wyman's study had similarities to the study conducted by Williams (2012). Some of the reasons indicated in the study leading to doctoral dropouts were a shift in personal situations, lack of financial resources, and difficulty with the doctoral program (Wyman, 2012). One similarity between the two studies was the disconnection doctoral students experienced with their chair or mentor. A lack of mentor support is detrimental to doctoral students trying to obtain degrees (Kennedy, Terrell, & Lohle, 2015). Results from Williams (2012) and Wyman (2012) studies showed different factors affecting students dropping out of the doctoral program. The key factor between the Williams and Wyman studies was the quality of the mentoring relationship. The findings of both acknowledged that lack of mentor support can result in doctoral students not completing their degrees.

---

[1] *Hermeneutic phenomenology: The hermeneutic approach of phenomenology assumes that participants have experienced the phenomenon being studied, that they view these experiences as conscious ones (van Manen, 1997)*

Other research studies have contrasting views on what have led doctoral students to drop out of the doctoral program. Pyhalto and Keskinen's (2012) qualitative study surveyed 668 doctoral candidates from three faculties of the University of Helsinki, Finland illustrated how a doctoral students' sense of relational agency[2] is related to the students' persistence in continuing to study at the doctoral level. Pyhalto and Keskinen (2012) conducted a study focusing on the exploration of doctoral students' sense of relational agency in terms of their scholarly communities. The scholarly community practices are important to the success of doctoral students. Doctoral student's involvement in these communities contribute to the doctoral experience (Gardner, 2010).

A significant factor determining the success of the doctoral student is the student themselves. According to Anderson and Anderson (2011), a student who takes on their own actions and have great internal self-direction are more likely not to drop out of the doctoral program. The findings in the study conducted by Pyhalto and Keskinen (2012) indicate proactive involvement in the scholarly communities reduces the risk of dropping out. The doctoral students own their own actions to success and when they do not, they are more prone to drop out.

Similar views were also indicated in a study conducted by Burmester, Metscher, and Smith (2014). Burmester's et al. (2014) quantitative study of 732 graduate online students and 476 undergraduate online students identified factors that interfered with successfully completing degrees through an online program. Obtaining doctorate degrees through an

---

[2] *Relational agency enables collaboration across different fields and various boundaries drawing resources from all fields.*

online forum is becoming more popular due to personal and financial convenience and students must remain disciplined to complete those online doctoral programs. Factors point to the academic learner as the problem.

One factor is student persistence where the student may have other priorities in the way of completing doctoral programs. Many students work for a living and balancing work and school may be too difficult (Burmester et al., 2014). Another factor noted by Burmester et al (2014) was technological limitations. Many students have the technical knowledge to use computers, but many were also easily distracted while doing classwork online. Many students used the Internet for access to non-academic sites while trying to do school work. Students selected in this study never used a support system to help them through difficult times.

Other studies continue to identify other human factors that inhibit doctoral student's completion of their degrees. Stallone's (2011) mix-method study of 140 doctoral students at two regional universities at Texas A&M University indicated doctoral students blame human factors; individual factors were not seen as a mitigating factor because individual factors are internal to the doctoral student. The mentor/mentee relationship was at the forefront and was considered the greatest predictor of degree completion Pena et al (2011). Stallone (2011) conducted the study using doctoral students from two different universities seeking to obtain personal perceptions on mentoring relationships. The study concluded that human factors such as student-faculty relationships was a key factor for doctoral program success.

Other studies were available on doctoral student mentoring, but none focused on perceptions of mentor relationships in doctoral programs. Studies including those by Yob and Crawford (2012) and Holley and Caldwell (2012) focused on conceptual frameworks for mentoring doctoral students, challenges of designing and implementing a mentoring program, and post marketing doctoral graduate's perception on mentoring training received. None of the relevant studies mentioned in this entire section focused or explored doctoral mentors' perceptions on mentoring relationship experiences and student compatibility in doctoral programs.

Yob and Crawford (2012) focused on conceptual frameworks for mentoring doctoral students by outlining four lines of inquiry around mentoring: (a) perceptions of successful mentoring, (b) how mentoring effects students with the dissertation process and research, (c) online environment of mentoring doctoral students, and (d) mentoring relationship behaviors between mentors and doctoral students. Yob and Crawford's conceptual model of identifying qualities contributing to successful mentoring included two main domains, academic and psychosocial, each providing different attributes to assist in the study. Each of the domains incorporated mentor behaviors and characteristics considered traditional. Associating with the academic domain, four characteristics were indicated as mentoring attributes. Yob and Crawford described these as: (a) competence, (b) availability, (c) induction, and (d) challenge. According to Yob and Crawford, mentors need to be competent, available to mentees, have the capabilities of inducting mentees into mentees respective professions, and must also challenge doctoral mentees.

The psychosocial domain included three characteristics indicated as mentoring attributes. Yob and Crawford described these three as: (a) personal qualities, (b) communication, and (c) emotional support. Certain qualities mentors have enabled doctoral students to become closer to their mentors. Yob and

Crawford described one of the personal qualities as trust. Trust was one of the most important qualities in the mentoring relationship (Stephenson & Christensen, 2007). Without trust, mentoring relationships could be disastrous. The second characteristic of the psychosocial domain included communication. A barrier in communication pairing could result in unfavorable outcomes for both mentors and mentees. Some of the outcomes could include confusion, distrust, and negative outcomes for the relationship (Evans, 2007). The last characteristic was emotional support. According to Forehand (2008), emotional support could have positive outcomes for mentors and produce self-sufficiency for doctoral students. After conducting the research and using seven attributes as the basis for the study, Yob and Crawford concluded the need for further research to extend, contrast, disconfirm, or confirm the seven attributes and two domains of the conceptual framework for mentoring doctoral students.

While Yob and Crawford (2012) focused on conceptual frameworks for mentoring doctoral students, Holley and Caldwell (2012) examined and explored the challenges of designing and implementing doctoral student mentoring programs. Holley and Caldwell's alternative view focused on faculty members, students, and peer mentors where each were brought together to introduce a team-based platform facilitating doctoral student success. Doctoral students' experiences and motivation, while in a formal mentoring program, was studied to seek understanding of the phenomena. Holly and Caldwell constructed three primary components of the mentoring program with one of the components being relationships between doctoral students and mentors. The study indicated a need for careful selection of doctoral mentors compatible to doctoral students. Holly and Caldwell found students had success pairing with mentors under the same academic discipline; mentoring relationships with different disciplines found building a mentor relationship to be difficult. Some other factors that positively influenced the mentoring relationship were personal characteristics such as age, race, and gender (Holly and Caldwell). Holley and Caldwell (2012) concluded several factors for a successful design and implementation of a doctoral mentoring program: the ability of students and faculty members to be mentors, doctoral student's interest in participating, and administrative efforts to initiate the efforts.

Gap in Literature

This exploratory, multiple-case study explored 10 doctoral mentors' perceptions on mentoring relationship experiences and student compatibility in doctoral programs. This study involved 10 doctoral mentors who mentor doctoral students from two different universities in the state of Delaware. No study was found in the reviewed literature on research conducted in this geographical location.

Several studies have been conducted on different components of mentoring doctoral students, none focused on exploring doctoral mentors' perceptions on mentoring relationship experiences and student compatibility in doctoral programs. An attempt was made to provide a deeper understanding by bridging the gap of mentors' perceptions when developing a mentoring relationship with doctoral students. Recent studies within five years of this research's publication have explored the subject of mentoring in doctoral programs, but these studies have failed to explore doctoral mentors' perceptions on mentoring relationship experiences and student compatibility in respective doctoral programs. One study conducted by Nakanjako et al (2014) included a cross-sectional, qualitative evaluation between 12 mentors and 22 doctoral students at Makerere University College in Uganda. This study was conducted as part of the monitoring and evaluation program for doctoral training at Makerere University College of Health Sciences. Though this study aimed at looking at how mentoring was being done, it was only limited to one case and student compatibility was never discussed, illustrating a gap between Nakanjakos' et al (2014) study and this study.

Theories illustrated by Lundgren and Orsillo (2012) discussed different opportunities for mentorship competence in formalized doctoral training programs. Lundgren and Orsillo also reflected on personal mentoring experiences in psychological discipline for doctoral training. The reflections and theories only illustrate the effects of mentoring experiences in one discipline. Lundgren and Orsillo fell short in bridging the gap on mentoring experiences across all disciplines and student compatibility across different cases.

Rayford (2014) used a qualitative analysis which explored mentoring experiences and perceptions of 20 female students enrolled in a doctoral program in education at Midwestern University. Though Rayford's study collected data on the perception of mentoring experiences by female students at Midwestern University, it was limited to specific demographical components. The components of Rayford's study only consist of female doctoral students and only including one organization, which is Midwestern University. Due to the limited demographical components studied, it left a gap in the available literature.

A qualitative study conducted by Columbaro (2015) explored mentoring relationships existence within online doctoral programs. Columbaro also explored 12 online doctoral graduates' perceptions on how mentoring relationships prepare them to become tenure-track faculty in four years. Columbaro's study left a gap in literature, because it did not touch on mentoring relationships across all disciplines. The study was only relevant to online doctoral graduates trying to become tenure-track faculty members in a four-year, time-frame. Columbaro's study did not examine perceptions of mentor/mentee mentoring relationships and how student compatibility plays a part of that relationship.

Waddell-Terry (2014) explored multiple mentoring relationships and how it supported progression and degree completion in a Doctorate of Education (Ed.D.) program. This study was limited to those doctoral students going through the Ed.D. doctoral program. Mentoring relationships was not examined across all academic disciplines. Mentor and mentee mentoring relationships was discussed, but only through the perceptions of Ed.D. doctoral students. Student compatibility was not explored, which left a gap in the currently available research literature.

Fowler (2013) used a qualitative approach examining the experiences of female African-American doctoral students in the Human Resource Development graduate program. Fowlers' (2013) study was similar to Rayfords' (2014) study, with the exception that Fowler was studying African-American females in one discipline, whereas Rayford studied females in general under any academic discipline. Just like Rayfords' study, Fowlers' study was limited to specific demographical components that excluded an exploration of student compatibility and mentoring relationships through multiple academic disciplines. Due to the limited demographical components studied it left a gap in the currently available literature.

General problems of mentorship practice often leave a gap between the mentoring policies intent and practices in educational institutions (Washburn-Moses, 2010). Gaps could potentially affect mentor relationship between mentors and doctoral students. This study was valuable, considering the gap in literature and limited recent research on mentors' perception of the mentor relationship in doctoral programs and student compatibility. This research study provided an opportunity to compare, and contrast, findings from previously conducted, relevant studies to enhance the literature and academic knowledge of mentoring relationships and Ph.D. student compatibility.

Conclusion

The literature review identified the importance of establishing an effective mentoring relationship between doctoral students and mentors. Mentor relationships at the doctoral level in any academic institution rely heavily on mentoring policies to be set in place (Froehlich, 2012). Academic leaders that built theoretical frameworks around mentoring programs could help academic institutions to determine ways to incorporate mentoring to current and future mentees (Dominguez & Hager, 2013). For the mentoring relationship to be successful, there must be a good fit between mentors and mentees (Hall & Maltby, 2013). Different approaches to mentoring are applied to mentoring relationships because of technological advances and the way some class work is delivered. Developing a mentoring relationship could have its challenges, which could consist of compatibility, lack of support, and unclear expectations. Academic institutions should incorporate a mentoring program where cultural influences were identified to effectively match mentors to mentees. These findings confirmed past research acknowledging if students experience a lack of support from their advisor or committee during the dissertation stage, it could result in non-completion of the program (Bair & Haworth, 1999; Fletcher, 2009; Green & Kluever, 1997; Lovitts & Nelson, 2000; Lovitts, 2001; Willis & Carmichael, 2011).

Summary

Chapter 2 presented a review of the research literature on a historical overview on mentoring, mentors at a glance, mentor relationship building, interpersonal relationships, mentoring at traditional and nontraditional schools, negative and positive impact on mentoring relationships, mentor characteristics, cultural influences, mentoring programs, and current gaps in literature. The literature was reviewed for germane and current findings on mentoring and the affects mentoring has on students pursuing doctorate degrees. Through the mentoring process, potential problems arise from a lack of a structured framework for mentoring doctoral students (Yob & Crawford, 2012). One of the key components of a successful experience for doctoral students was the relationship developed between mentor and mentee (Holley & Caldwell, 2012).

The review of literature was used to support the purpose of this exploratory multiple-case study, to explore doctoral mentors' perceptions on mentoring relationship experiences and student compatibility in doctoral programs. In Chapter 3 the methodology of the study was discussed. Chapter 3 also presented the rationale for the method and design of the research, population, instruments, and validity.

Chapter 3

Method

The purpose of this exploratory, multiple-case study was to explore doctoral mentors' perceptions on mentoring relationship experiences and student compatibility in doctoral programs. Chapter 3 discussed in detail the research method and design appropriateness. A detailed description of the method to explore the perceptions of 10 doctoral mentors from two universities in the state of Delaware was also discussed. Provosts, academic deans, and doctoral chairs may use the results of this study when making changes to current mentoring programs.

Research Method and Design Appropriateness

Research Method

This qualitative, exploratory, multiple-case study explored doctoral mentors' perceptions on mentoring relationship experiences and student compatibility in doctoral programs. Investigating the process of experiences, qualitative researchers attempted to interpret the experiences to make meaning of the experience (Townsend, Cox, & Li, 2010). Qualitative studies focused on the interpretation and meaning participants provided on experiences (Merriam, 2009).

Both qualitative and quantitative research methods contained strengths and weaknesses. Data collected through qualitative research derived from focus groups, interviews, documents, and direct observation that could have determined the how and why a phenomenon may exist (Dunnagan, Peterson, & Wilson, 1997). According to Patton (1990), researchers took an in-depth and detailed approach to an issue when they used qualitative methods. Choosing a qualitative method over a quantitative method was more appropriate for this study to gain insight into the perceptions of mentoring and student compatibility (Baxter & Jack, 2008).

Qualitative inquiry was naturalistic for exploring narrative real-life situations, instead of studying information solely based on predetermined constraints (Schempp, 1987). Qualitative researchers explored in-depth participants' perspectives, behaviors, and life experiences (Holloway & Wheeler, 2002). Qualitative researchers used in-depth, investigative parameters to discover the complications of participants' experiences through a holistic structure (Holloway & Wheeler, 2002). Qualitative inquiry also included an inductive analysis into theories about happenings within a setting, rather than deductive theories derived by hypothesis (Broughton, 1991).

A quantitative research study was not appropriate for this research study because unlike qualitative research, quantitative research studies collected numerical data to answer research questions (Christensen, Johnson & Turner, 2011). Answers from open-ended questions were collected in the form of non-numerical data consistent with qualitative research (Christensen et al., 2011). Quantitative studies measured variables of interest, whereas qualitative studies consisted of examining certain characteristics that may be impossible to show as a numerical value (Leedy & Ormrod,

2010). This qualitative study focused on an in-depth perspective of mentoring relationships between mentors and mentees.

Design Appropriateness

This qualitative exploratory study design was appropriate for exploring themes on perceptions of doctoral mentors' role in mentoring and student compatibility. This qualitative exploratory study was aligned with studying factors impacting mentoring relationships and focused on '*how*' questions of inquiry, which may identify themes, patterns, and new discoveries from the mentoring experience between doctoral students and mentors. According to Yin (2014), "*how*" questions of inquiry were geared more towards a case study design. The approach to this exploratory research study was selected to focus on the perceptions of doctoral mentors' role in mentoring and student compatibility.

Different research designs could be used when conducting a qualitative research study. Choosing the appropriate design depended on what the researcher is attempting to accomplish and the information sought from the study. One traditional, qualitative research, design that researchers considered was an ethnographic research study. Observations were at the core of ethnographic research requiring researchers to be placed within the contextual framework of the study (Willis, 2007). The researcher conducting an ethnographic study lives the experience of the participants understanding the participants' attitudes by taking field notes (Howcroft & McDonald, 2007). Ethnographic research also paid attention to discovery and description of a specific culture (Christensen et al., 2011). This qualitative, multiple-case study did not involve observing cultures and attitudes of selected participants, which made ethnographic research inappropriate to use.

Another traditional qualitative research design that was considered for use was 'grounded theory,' in which one or multiple hypotheses were developed after collecting relevant data to the study (Leedy & Ormrod, 2010). Grounded theory relied on prior empirical data systematically analyzed and did not begin from theoretical frameworks, as data collected would build theory (Gasson & Waters, 2013; Leedy & Ormrod, 2010). This qualitative, exploratory research study involved initially building theoretical frameworks on mentoring relationship(s). Previous research on doctoral mentoring relationships was examined by separating relevant and irrelevant information, thus grounded theory was inappropriate for this study.

A third qualitative research design considered by this researcher was a phenomenological study. Humans have perceptions of the surrounding world; a phenomenological study explored an in-depth understanding of human perspectives of a situation and/or specific phenomena (Willis, 2007; Leedy & Ormrod, 2010). Lived experiences from participants were not attempted or investigated, yet instead explored factors were integrated in the mentoring relationship described and how the mentoring relationship affects the participants' completion or non-completion rates within the associated doctoral programs. This qualitative multiple-case research study was not focused on describing the meaning of the experiences of the phenomenon, but instead revealed new insight (Leedy & Ormrod, 2010), thus a phenomenological study was not suitable.

This qualitative, exploratory, multiple-case study explored doctoral mentors' perception on the role of mentoring and student compatibility in doctoral programs through interview questions relating to the experiences of research participants during the mentoring relationship. In-depth interview questions were used to gather information needed on the perceptions of research participants. Analysis of participant responses helped determine themes and patterns of mentoring relationship development and to gain a better understanding of mentoring relationships (Stake, 1995).

Research Questions

The questions presented to selected participants were open-ended, which had a direct reflection on the purpose statement: to explore doctoral mentors' perceptions on mentoring relationship experiences and student compatibility in doctoral programs. Open-ended questions helped participants develop conversational tones that led to participants telling a story of experiences of mentoring doctoral students.

This research study focused on one central question and two sub-questions. The research question was as follows:

R1: How do doctoral mentors perceive the role of student mentoring and student compatibility in doctoral programs?

The following sub-questions guided the development of this qualitative research study and provided a foundation for developing the interview questions for the participants:

S1: How do doctoral mentors perceive the importance of the initiation phase of a mentor/mentee relationship?

S2: How do doctoral mentors perceive the importance of mentee cognitive development during the mentor/mentee relationship?

Population and Sampling

Doctoral mentors from two universities in the state of Delaware were asked to participate in this qualitative multiple-case study. The universities public online directory was used to find and create a list of potential participants that can be used. Potential participants had to meet unique criteria to be considered for the study, as stated on the informed consent (see Appendix B). Each potential participant meeting the criteria within the informed consent form (see Appendix B) received an invitation e-mail (see Appendix C) to participate in the research study. The first five qualified, potential participants to respond from each university were e-mailed an informed consent form (see Appendix B).

The number of selected participants were derived from a need to triangulate data obtained from several sources to form a better understanding of the mentoring relationship experienced by doctoral mentors with mentees. Ten doctoral mentor participants provided a diverse population from different universities to provide a deeper understanding of mentorship practices. Electing to conduct a qualitative research study produced a higher level of detailed information from a smaller sample of research participants (Patton, 1990). According to Patton (1990), a purposeful smaller sample selection increased the understanding of an issue under investigation.

Data collected from participants were strategized by using purposeful sampling (Baxter & Jack, 2008). Incorporating purposeful sampling provided the study with more credibility, trustworthiness, and overall quality (Baxter & Jack, 2008). The mentors selected had first-hand knowledge of the mentoring experience with mentees. Each mentor selected had three or more years of experience mentoring doctoral students as stated in the informed consent form (see Appendix B). The data collected from participants represented individual perceptions describing the experiences of establishing a mentoring relationship. This purposeful sampling provided the best information needed to investigate mentoring relationships because participants had experienced the phenomena first hand (Leedy & Ormrod, 2010). Selecting a smaller sample size decreased generalization to other issues (Dunnagan et al., 1997).

Informed Consent

Participants selected for this qualitative exploratory study were informed of any risks and or conditions associated with the research study through an informed consent form (see Appendices A and B) (Yin, 2014). The informed consent form provided participants information on any perceived risks, rights to privacy, guaranteed anonymity, the right to withdraw at any time without repercussions, and important contact information (Miller, 2014). Informed consent involved accountability of the researcher, regarding, and respecting each participant of the study. The process of informed consent involved giving participants the opportunity to determine participation in the study (Erlen, 2010). Participants for this qualitative, exploratory, multiple-case study received an invitation for participation through e-mail (see Appendix C). The e-mail list was generated from the two universities public roster of doctoral mentors and personal contacts.

Two doctoral mentors from two universities in the state

of Delaware with doctoral programs were invited to participate in a field test to test the validity and reliability of the interview questions. Using a field test tested the feasibility and research method on a smaller scale (Teijlingen & Hundley, 200). A field test gained feedback on the appropriateness of the interview questions being asked and did not answer the questions. The next five participants from each university to respond to the letter of invitation were invited to participate in the actual study.

Once participants were identified for the field test and actual research study they were provided an explanation of the process within the informed consent form (see Appendices A and B) and given an opportunity to ask any questions or concerns about the study. The informed consent forms were e-mailed to all participants and after all questions and concerns were addressed, the participants were asked to provide a scanned copy of a signature on the informed consent form. Once the signed consent forms from the 10 respondents were received, the participants were scheduled for the interview process.

Research participants participated on a voluntary basis. Each participant for the field test and actual study were informed of personal rights to withdraw the consent at any time before, during, or after the interviews. Participants were given the opportunity to disclose the intent to withdraw verbally or by written communication. Contact information was provided on the informed consent form (see Appendices A and B) and the letter of invitation (see Appendix D) for research participants.

Confidentiality

Confidentiality was important in this qualitative, exploratory, multiple-case study to increase the likelihood participants from the two selected universities responded honestly to the in-depth open-ended interview questions. The Informed Consent Letter (see Appendices A and B) explained the guaranteed confidentiality and purpose of the research study. Each participant's name and university remained confidential and known only to the researcher. To ensure anonymity and confidentiality, each university and participant from the audio recording and transcript had an alpha-numeric code. Anonymous codes were used in place of the individuals' name and the two associated universities.

Participants included in the research were reminded that participation was strictly confidential and voluntary. Each participant had a chance to withdraw from the study before, during, or after data was collected without any penalties, as stated on the informed consent form (see Appendices A and B). The request to withdraw was to be sent through an e-mail identified on the informed consent form. A confirmation e-mail would have been sent back to participants who wanted to withdraw. Any data collected from participants wanting to withdraw would have been shredded and destroyed. The confirmation e-mail would have stated how data collected from the withdrawing participant would have been destroyed.

Participants included in the research were encouraged to make contact by e-mail or phone if there were any questions pertaining to confidentiality, which was stated on informed consent form (see Appendices A and B). All data collected was protected and stored in a locked secured space and remained so for three years, after which all data will be destroyed. After three years, the data collected, interview notes, and tape recordings would be appropriately destroyed.

Data Collection

Data collection for this qualitative research study was conducted through in-depth, open-ended interview questions. According to Leedy and Ormrod (2010) interviews could produce a great amount of useful information from participants. The use of an in-depth interview method was used to collect data on the perceptions and experiences of doctoral mentors' role of mentoring and student compatibility in doctoral programs from two selected universities in the state of Delaware (University of Delaware and Wilmington University).

The open-ended interview process in this exploratory, multiple-case study consisted of recording the session with a tape-recorder and taking notes. According to Leedy and Ormrod (2010) qualitative researchers should record useful data that could potentially help in the research study.

As the data were collected through the interview, notes were taken on the initial interpretation of answers from the research participant. The data collection interview took place in a private and safe environment where only the interviewer and interviewee was present. Each interview lasted approximately 30 to 45 minutes in length. The interviewees were asked questions to elicit responses on perceptions and experiences of mentoring and student compatibility in doctoral programs. The following steps were used for primary data collection:

1. Each participant was briefed of the nature of the study and was asked to think about the mentoring relationship experience with doctoral students.

2. Open-ended questions (see Appendix D) were asked and participant responses were tape-recorded by the researcher.

After the interview and transcription of the interviews had been completed, a transcription of the recorded interview was provided to each participant to ensure the information recorded was authenticated, accurate, and no answers had been manipulated. Transcript verification was appropriate to ensure data collected were consistent. The research sent a copy of transcribed recorded interview via email to each participant for quality assurance and review. The following interview questions were asked to capture themes and patterns on doctoral mentors' role as a mentor:

1. How would you describe your role as a mentor in recent years?
2. How do you perceive your role as a doctoral mentor?
3. How important is the early phase of building a mentoring relationship with a mentee? Please elaborate and provide examples.
4. What type of indications and factors are associated with building an effective mentoring relationship during the initiation phase?
5. How important is cognitive development (i.e. writing, research skills, and developing new learning patterns) in mentees during the mentor/mentee relationship? Please elaborate.

6. How do you think a mentor's positive influence affects a mentee's cognitive development?
7. How do you think a mentor's lack of positive influence affect the cognitive development of mentees?

The following interview questions were asked to capture themes and patterns on the doctoral mentor's experience and perception on the mentor/mentee matching process:

What are your feelings on the mentor/mentee matching process currently used at your university?

How does the university ensure compatibility when matching doctoral students with mentors?

The following interview question was asked to capture themes and patterns on the doctoral mentors' perception on ways to improve the mentor/mentee relationship:

What would help improve mentoring relationships?

The following interview question was asked to capture themes and patterns on anything that has not been discussed to add more rich data to the study on mentoring relationships:

Is there anything you can add to this discussion and study we have not touched on?

Field Test

Field tests are used for a variety of reasons, but they do not substitute the process of collecting primary data. The first stage of this research was conducting a field test by selecting four doctoral mentors with three or more years doctoral mentoring experience from two universities in the state of Delaware. In qualitative research, the validity and reliability of questions cannot be statistically tested, so researchers typically field test the instrument. Conducting a field test involved sending the interview questions to experienced doctoral mentors to test the validity and appropriateness of the interview questions being asked. Results of the field test was used to validate appropriateness of the interview questions. The results also consisted of making modifications to the interview questions necessary for continuance with the research study. No additional research-related data was collected from field test participants.

Each potential participant meeting the criteria within the informed consent form (see Appendix A) received an invitation e-mail (see Appendix E) to participate in the field test. The first two potential participants that responded from each university were selected to conduct the field test and sent via e-mail an informed consent form (see Appendix A). Once the informed consent forms were received back from each field test participant via e-mail, a separate e-mail was sent to schedule a date to send the interview questions for review to conduct the field test. The intent of the field test was to gain feedback on the appropriateness of the interview questions being asked – not to answer the questions. Feedback from field test participants was not included in data analysis of actual research study.

Instrumentation

Qualitative researchers collected data, analyzed the data found, and interpreted the results, which allowed for a report of the findings (Christensen et al., 2011). One of the major methods of data collection was interviews, where an interviewer will ask the interviewee a variety of questions (Christensen et al., 2011). In case study design, interviews were an essential source because human experiences and behaviors could be used as evidence (Yin, 2009). The use of the in-depth interview method was used to collect data on the perceptions and experiences of doctoral mentors mentoring relationship with doctoral students.

The open-ended interview process in this exploratory, multiple-case study consisted of recording the session with a tape-recorder and taking notes. The interview began with the introduction of each participant, and participants were informed the open-ended interview questions (see Appendix D) were intended to elicit responses on mentoring relationships experienced with doctoral students. The participants were asked to elaborate on the role of mentoring and student compatibility in doctoral programs. Participants were also informed the right to withdraw at any time without repercussion (see Appendices A and B).

To ensure an understanding and clarity of the interview questions, a field test occurred with four doctoral mentors to examine and validate the initial research questions. Data collected from field test participants provided evidence of the feasibility of using the initial interview questions. Data collected also provided evidence that some of the interview questions were not adequate and more follow-up questions were needed to obtain all required data.

Dependability, Credibility, and Transferability

Qualitative research was designed to understand perspectives of individuals providing insight into the experiences individuals had (Rowan & Huston, 1997). One researcher may comprehend qualitative research differently than another researcher (Cao, 2007). All researchers must establish trustworthiness in research studies (Cao, 2007).

Trustworthiness could be obtained by establishing dependability and credibility (Sinkovics, Penz, & Ghauri, 2008). Dependability and credibility influenced confidence in qualitative research (Munn et al., 2014). Quantitative researchers were more concerned with the fundamentals of reliability and validity (Sinkovics et al., 2008).

Dependability

According to Sinkovics et al. (2008) reliability in quantitative research is equivalent to dependability in qualitative research. A research study's consistency or stability coming from measurement instrument scores refers to the research's reliability (Drost, 2011). Measuring something accurately was accomplished when it could be measured consistently (Leedy & Ormrod, 2010). Adding to research reliability was the task of conducting a field test to confirm consistency and ensure everything asked was focused on clarity (Makewa, Role, & Tuguta, 2013). Research questions in the field test were tested for appropriateness for this qualitative study. Measuring something consistently does guarantee increased accuracy, which meant the reliability of research data was necessary, but was a separate condition for validity (Leedy & Ormrod, 2010).

Credibility

Measurement instruments are important in qualitative research and should measure what is intended to be measured. Measuring only those elements that need to be measured creates validity of the research (Leedy & Ormrod, 2010). A measurement instrument's validity is specific to the type of study being conducted (Leedy & Ormrod, 2010). Interviews produce moderately high measurement validity when questions asked to the research participants are properly constructed and validated (Christensen et al., 2011). One factor that will influence validity is truthfulness (Neuman, 2011). Participants were asked to be truthful since qualitative researchers are looking for authenticity by providing an honest, fair, and balanced account of perceptions (Neuman, 2011). NVivo 11 software was used to organize and process collected data from each participant during the actual research study.

A threat or concern to trustworthiness with the study were participants not being honest with answers provided in the interview. Participants must be trusted and trustworthiness depended on the researchers' credibility (Merriam, 2009). The study was conducted in an ethical manner. The study showed IRB-approved research procedures were faithfully followed (Firestone, 1987). Participants felt more comfortable to answer truthfully during the interview process, which made the study more credible.

Bias and prejudices were explored and avoided before conducting any interviews and after the interview was concluded. Prior, during, and after the interview, biases were explored through bracketing. Researchers using bracketing set aside and refrained from pre-conceptions or assumptions about the research study (Al-Natour et al., 2015).

Because researchers may have emotional ties to the study, researchers using bracketing helped to prevent the researcher from manipulating any data collected (Tufford & Newman, 2010). To avoid other bias, tape-recorded interviews were played multiple times during transcription to ensure transcription was accurate without adding or deleting anything stated during the interview.

To increase the credibility and validity of research results, triangulation of multiple data sources was used. According to Yin (2014), the strength of collecting data in case studies was the use of different sources of evidence. The theoretical framework, participants' review of interview responses, and audio-tape recording of the interview process established triangulation. The theories used for triangulation were mentor relationship, initiation, cognitive development, and mentoring relationship impact. The data collected should have the ability to be replicated for other researchers to replicate the same process (Yin, 2014).

Transferability

In qualitative studies, researchers argued the need for validity, whereas quantitative researchers expect validity. In quantitative research, external validity was achieved when the same methodology could be applied to another set of samples and produce similar results (Merriam, 2009). External validity was not required in qualitative research because each research was different and provided different settings. Achieving validity in qualitative research was dependent upon transferability (Trochim, 2006). Transferability was the ability to generalize and show how the study outcomes could be used and applied to other situations (Shank, 2006). Transferability was used in qualitative studies to make connections between study elements and personal experiences (Wahyuni, 2012). To ensure transferability was also possible, descriptive data must be present within the study (Lincoln & Guba, 1985). The findings in this study served as foundational information that may be transferable to other academic institutions outside the state of Delaware.

Data Analysis

Common themes and patterns on doctoral mentors' perceptions of the role as a mentor and student compatibility was examined. Answers from the research participants were manually transcribed from a digital, audio, voice-recorder and uploaded into NVivo 11; data analysis software. NVivo11 was used in data reduction to enable the coding and analysis of the text and audio results from the interviews with participants. NVivo was a computer-based, data-analysis tool used in qualitative research to analyze contents and enhance the data-analysis process from the responses of the interview with participants (NVivo, 2013). NVivo 11 streamlined the data and helped facilitate understanding of unstructured data. During the data analysis process, transcribing the data was the first step (Wainwright & Russell, 2010). Paying close attention to one interview at a time assisted in noticing any unanticipated situations (Bailey, 2008).

After analyzing each case, a cross-case analysis was used to identify the overarching themes and patterns across each case. A cross-case analysis consisted of investigating themes and patterns. Researchers using cross-case analysis helped to identify similarities and differences about each case, (Stake, 2006). The cases were reviewed with the known quintain to develop themes and patterns. Stake's (2006) cross-case analysis procedure consisted of review of each case from collected data to identify prominent themes and patterns.

NVivo 11 software was used to group phrases and words creating common themes and patterns to discover terms frequently used from the interview. Coding consisted of organizing and sorting collected data to summarize and synthesize the data. Codes were set up in different categories that involved words, phrases, or numbers after systematically going through the interview transcript (Glaser & Laudel, 2013). Themes, ideas, and concepts were coded to fit the different categories. Common themes and patterns were identified until saturation was reached. According to Morse (1995), when no new information could be obtained from qualitative data, saturation had been reached.

Summary

This qualitative, exploratory, multiple-case study involved exploring doctoral mentors' perceptions on mentoring relationship experiences and student compatibility in doctoral programs. The chapter presented the rationale for using a qualitative, exploratory, multiple-case study design. This qualitative research method and design was appropriate for this research study because it involved exploring how 10 doctoral mentors perceive the role of mentoring and student compatibility in doctoral programs at two selected universities in the state of Delaware. This purposeful sampling provided a diverse population from different universities to show how mentorship practice was experienced from selected participants.

Data was collected using a semi structured interview. The in-depth interview in this case study were recorded and transcribed to analyze results from the interview with participants. Answers from the research participants were transcribed and uploaded into data analysis coding software called NVivo11. After analyzing each case, a cross-case analysis was used to identify the overarching themes and patterns across each case. Chapter 4 detailed the results of the research study after the data collection process and analysis of the data, which was interpreted for understanding.

Chapter 4

Results

The purpose of this exploratory, multiple-case study was to explore doctoral mentors' perceptions on mentoring relationship experiences and student compatibility in doctoral programs. Face-to-face interviews allowed for qualitative data collection that represented personal perspectives of doctoral mentors' perception on mentoring doctoral students and student compatibility. This study was significant because new data were generated regarding doctoral mentors' perception associated with mentoring doctoral students in doctoral programs. Data collected could be used by provosts, academic deans, and doctoral chairs to evaluate or form a basis for updated / upgraded / improved mentoring processes in doctoral programs. Institutional leaders may also be able to provide improved or realigned mentorship practices addressing doctoral students learning needs, thus possibly increasing doctoral student completion rates.

One research question and two sub-questions formed the basis of inquiry used to solicit responses from doctoral mentors and were as follows:

R1: How do doctoral mentors perceive the role of student mentoring and student compatibility in doctoral programs?

S1: How do doctoral mentors perceive the importance of the initiation phase of a mentor/mentee relationship?

S2: How do doctoral mentors perceive the importance of mentee cognitive development during the mentor/mentee relationship?

Chapter 4 included the results and findings of the study, and analysis of 10 participant interviews with doctoral mentors from two universities in the state of Delaware. Chapter 4 provided a detailed description of the data collection and identification of themes and patterns.

Data Collection Process

The data collection process was done in two stages. In the first stage, a field test was conducted to capture feedback from four doctoral mentors having three or more years of experience mentoring doctoral students. A field test was conducted to start the research process by establishing qualitative research protocol and validating the original interview questions. Subject matter expertise from field test participants helped the researcher to add, remove, revise, and validate interview questions. The second stage of the data collection process was conducted with 10 participants. In each stage, all participants gave written informed consent.

Field Test

Prior to conducting the actual interviews for this study, a field test was used to test the validity and appropriateness of the interview questions being asked. In qualitative research the validity and reliability of questions cannot be statistically tested so researchers typically field test the instrument (University of Phoenix, 2015). According to University of

Phoenix (2015) field experts tested the instrument to aid in refining or improving the interview questions. The field test participants included four doctoral mentors with three or more years doctoral mentoring experience from two universities in the state of Delaware.

Each participant meeting the criteria within the informed consent form (see Appendix A) received an invitation e-mail (see Appendix E) to participate in the field test. The first two participants that responded from each university were selected and sent an informed consent form via e-mail (see Appendix A). Once informed consent forms were received from each participant, a copy of the interview questions was sent to participants via email to review and provide feedback. Each field test participant reviewed the original interview questions and provided feedback with changes, modifications, additions, or deletions to the instrument. The field test took approximately two weeks to complete.

Changes to Field Test Interview Questions

Input from the four, field-test participants confirmed the need to modify the interview questions for better understanding, with an exception of one interview question (question #2). The original set of interview questions consisted of 10 questions (see Appendix F).

The first question, 'How do you perceive your role as a mentor in general?' was to gain an idea of how participants saw themselves as not only a doctoral mentor, but as a mentor to others. This was important as it relates to different aspects of being a mentor. There could be a difference in being a mentor to a doctoral student and being a mentor to non-doctoral students. One field-test respondent expressed that the term, in general, should be removed. Another field-test respondent suggested adding a time qualifier to the question. Adding a time qualifier meant the researcher could obtain participant's perspectives for a specific time-period.

The third question, 'How important is the initiation phase of building a mentoring relationship with a mentee?' was to explore the importance of building a mentoring relationship from the beginning when mentees first meet mentors to begin the doctoral process. Several field-test participants thought this was a good question. One field-test participant suggested the researcher change initiation phase to early phase since the term initiation can take on different meanings. Another field-test participant suggested the researcher ask the interviewee to elaborate and provide examples to gain richer data.

The fourth question, 'What type of indication(s) is associated with being a good fit when building an effective mentoring relationship during the initiation phase?' meant to explore what it takes to build a good mentoring relationship when mentees first meet their mentors. The question looked at finding different indicators associated with establishing a positive relationship. One field-test participant suggested a change to the question to reflect on building an effective mentoring relationship rather than being a good fit.

The fifth question, 'How important is cognitive development in mentees during the mentor/mentee relationship?' was to explore how doctoral students develop new learning patterns going through the doctoral process. Learning patterns include writing and research skills. One field-test participant stated cognitive development was too broad and should be narrowed down. The other field-test participants stated this question was unclear and the term cognitive development needed to be defined to participants before the interview starts.

The sixth question, 'How do you think a mentor's influence enhances a mentees cognitive development?' was to explore how the actions of mentors help or hinder the mentees ability in dissertation writing, research, and developing new learning patterns during the doctoral process. One field-test participant felt the term *'enhances'* was a biased word and suggested a change. The remaining field-test participants reiterated the need for the term cognitive development be defined.

The seventh question, 'What are your feelings on the lack of a mentor's positive influence that may inhibit the cognitive development of mentees?' was to explore how a mentor's lack of positive influence can affect a mentee's learning development. The exploration was intended to show positive and negative effects of learning. Several field-test participants suggested the term cognitive development be defined. Another field-test participant stated the question was too wordy and confusing.

The eighth question, 'What do you remember most about your experiences with the matching of a mentee?' was to explore participants' experiences with the mentor/mentee matching process currently being used in the particular university where the study was being performed. One field-test participant thought this question was too broad. Another field-test participant suggested adding the specific place the mentoring process was taking place.

The ninth question, 'What are your feelings on the mentor/mentee matching process?' was to explore participant's perception on the mentor/mentee matching process. Field-test participants were fine with this interview question with only one suggestion. One field-test participant suggested including the process currently being used in the university to show the question is being directed to the university the actual participant is affiliated with.

The tenth question, 'How do you ensure compatibility when matching with a doctoral student?' was to explore how participants make sure they are compatible to mentees they select or are assigned to. Field-test participants thought this was a good question as compatibility is often an important topic when matching mentors to mentees. Field-test participants suggested the researcher revise the first part of the question to reflect how the university ensures compatibility versus how the mentor ensures compatibility.

Based on the recommendations of the field test participants, the interview question revisions included several additional questions (see Appendix F). One added interview question reflected on ways to improve mentoring relationships and another question was added to expand on anything left out the participant felt was important to discuss. One field test participant felt the added feedback collected on the additional questions would be adequate to address the research question of the actual study. The field test participants did not take part in the actual study. Information and feedback collected in the field test was not included in the actual research study or data analysis.

Data Collection

The participant goal for this research study was to interview 10 doctoral mentors from two universities in the state of Delaware; five from one university and five from the other university. Semi-structured, face-to-face interviews were conducted, collecting rich, descriptive doctoral mentors' perception on mentoring relationship experiences and student compatibility in doctoral programs. Prior to starting the interview, each participant submitted a signed informed consent form which included an agreement to be audio-recorded. The interviews lasted 45 to 60 minutes in a safe and private location. As a convenience, doctoral mentors were provided the opportunity to be interviewed at the academic institution or a public library in a conference room for anonymity and privacy. Of the 10 doctoral mentors, one took place at a public library and the remaining nine were held at the academic institution where the doctoral mentor provided a private place to be interviewed.

Interviews included open-ended interview questions allowing participants to direct the conversation with various perspectives. Objective follow up questions were asked on numerous occasions to clarify specific experiences, thoughts, and feelings related to the answers participants provided. Each doctoral mentor approved the use of a handheld audio recorder. The audio-recorded data was then transcribed, leading to textual data used to capture common themes and patterns. Participant interviews resulted in 68 pages (total) of transcribed data. After the interview and transcription of the interviews was completed, a transcription of the unique to each participant's recorded interview was provided to each participant to ensure the information recorded was authenticated, accurate, and that no answers had been manipulated. Transcript verification was appropriate to ensure data collected were consistent. An email of the transcribed recorded interview was sent to each participant by the researcher. The data collection process took place over a 3-week time-period.

Participant Coding

A participant coding system was created manually to protect the privacy and confidentiality of the academic institutions and study participants. W1 through W5 represented doctoral mentors from case S1 (see Table 2). D1 through D5 represented doctoral mentors from case S2 (see Table 2).

Table 2 - Demographics

Participant	Case	Position	Gender	Teaching Experience	Mentoring Experience	Race	Age
W1	S1	Mentor	Female	18 years	7 years	African-American	40-49
W2	S1	Mentor	Female	16 years	5 years	Caucasian	50-59
W3	S1	Mentor	Male	26 years	20 years	Caucasian	70-79
W4	S1	Mentor	Female	25 years	13 years	Caucasian	60-69
W5	S1	Mentor	Female	11 years	3 years	Caucasian	50-59
D1	S2	Mentor	Male	16 years	8 years	Caucasian	40-49
D2	S2	Mentor	Male	23 years	6 years	Caucasian	70-79
D3	S2	Mentor	Female	14 years	7 years	Caucasian	40-49
D4	S2	Mentor	Female	13 years	8 years	Caucasian	40-49
D5	S2	Mentor	Male	26 years	10 years	African-American	50-59

Demographic Information of Cases

In the current research study, the demographic data was used to illustrate total number of years teaching at the college level, total years of mentoring doctoral students, race of participants, and age of participants. Demographic data was collected before the actual interview started. There were 10 participants in this qualitative multiple-case study (see Table 2). There was a mixture of male and female participants (see Table 2). S1 and S2 each included five mentors (see Table 2). The demographic data supported the original proposal that included participants being selected based on experience level of mentoring doctoral students.

Years of Teaching Experience

In S1 and S2, participants reported the number of years of teaching experience. The teaching experience ranged from 11 to 26 years (see table 2). In S1 two mentors had between 25 and 26 years teaching experience and three mentors had between 11 to 18 years teaching experience. In S2 two mentors had between 23 and 26 years teaching experience and three mentors had between 13 to 16 years teaching experience (see Table 2). The mentors participating in this study had a lot of experience teaching at the college level. Teaching experience data was used to enhance the description of the cases

Years of Doctoral Mentoring Experience

In S1 and S2, participants reported the number of years of mentoring doctoral student's experience. The mentoring experience ranged from 3 to 20 years (see table 2).

In S1 two mentors had between 13 and 20 years of mentoring experience and three mentors had between 3 to 7 years mentoring experience. In S2 one mentor had 10 years mentoring experience and four mentors had between 6 to 8 years mentoring experience (see Table 2). The mentors participating in this study had a diverse range of mentoring experience of doctoral students. The mentoring of doctoral students' data was used to enhance the description of the cases.

Ethnicity

Of the five participants in S1, 80% were identified as Caucasian and 20% was identified as African-American (see Table 2). In S2, 80% were identified as Caucasian and 20% was identified as African-American (see Table 2).

Age of Participants

Both S1 and S2 participant's age ranged from 40 to 79 years old (see Table 2). When viewing both cases holistically, 40% of participants ranged in age from 40 to 49, 30% ranged in age from 50 to 59, 10% ranged in age from 60-69, and 20% ranged in age from 70-79 (see Table 2).

Data Analysis

Data analysis began with a goal of capturing themes and patterns within the interviews from study participants. Answers from the research participants was manually transcribed from a digital, audio, voice-recorder and uploaded into NVivo 11; data analysis software searching for themes and patterns. After analyzing each case, a cross-case analysis was used to identify the overarching themes and patterns across each case. Themes, patterns, and expressions from each participant was analyzed exploring participants' perceptions on mentoring relationships and student compatibility in doctoral programs. NVivo 11 software grouped phrases and words creating common themes and patterns to discover terms frequently used from the interview. Each participant responded to 11 interview questions and all answers provided data for the research. Themes, ideas, and concepts were coded to fit the different categories. Common themes and patterns were identified until saturation was reached. When no new information can be obtained from qualitative data, saturation has been reached (Morse, 1995).

Emerging Themes

Emerging themes were collected and organized from the manual transcription of each participant interview. The findings produced several core themes from the 11 interview questions: (a) cognitive development, (b) improvements, (c) indicators and factors, (d) influence, (e) matching process, (f) perceptions, (g) relationships, (h) role, and (i) student networking. Each research study participant described their perceptions on mentoring relationships and student compatibility in doctoral programs. The use of NVivo 11 software was utilized to categorize and arrange themes (see Table 3).

Table 3 - Frequency of Core Themes Mentioned by Participants

Core Themes	Participants who mentioned theme during interviews (n)	Total mention of themes by any participant during interviews (N)
1. Cognitive Development	10	39
2. Matching Process	10	45
3. Indicators and Factors	10	27
4. Influence	10	37
5. Student Networking	3	8
6. Role	10	21
7. Relationships	9	36
8. Perceptions	10	28
9. Improvements	9	39

Theme 1 – Cognitive Development

Cognitive development was defined for this research study as doctoral students' ability to learn new knowledge during the doctoral journey. Cognitive development was also defined as a doctoral students' capability of knowing how to conduct research and writing a dissertation under the direction of their doctoral mentor. Cognitive development was considered as an importance to mentor/mentee relationships and considered on how a mentor's positive or negative influence can affect doctoral students. Participants from both cases agreed that cognitive development was important during the mentor/mentee relationship. Participant D1 from the first case stated, "Students will have to learn how to adapt to changes and learn new ways of doing things when it comes to writing the dissertation and doing research". Participant D2 maintained,

> "The way you are defining it, I think is majorly importantly, huge, because in the cases of doctoral interns, they're going to be working on or working toward dissertation towards studies. They would need to be able to think through with support. Think through an idea or proposal. Something they could be enthusiastic about. Something that was doable. I would sometimes help them to break down their objectives. I would ask, "What are the criteria for you for what you want to study? What are the most important criteria?" Narrowing it down. Helping them to narrow down an idea."

In terms of cognitive development being important in a mentor/mentee relationship D3 stated,

> It is hard to separate that out, because if you are a doctoral student(s), you better have those things. If you do not, that sends up a bit of a red flag for me in terms of why are you here and how did you get here. In terms of the mentor- mentee relationship, how 'Let's see here. How important it is in that relationship?' I think it should be a given at that point. If its not there, that's concerning to me, because this is doctoral level education. If you're not at that stage I guess stumped on the question, because if I were to meet someone who had some issues in that area, I would have to dial

> it back and say, "What's going on?" I'd almost have to go to my program director and say, "How did this student get here?" Because they're not going to succeed in the program if their cognitive development is not up to par.

In case number two, W2 goes a little deeper with cognitive development by playing simple games to help students understand the dissertation process. W2 stated,

> I think I am the only one that teaches that course who uses that, although I shared it with a couple of other instructors. I do not think they used it, because I do not think they're comfortable with it. Having taught high school and having played games on a computer, showing the student this is what its all about, and I do that with my undergraduates in my science classes. I go on there and do simulations all the time. What if you do this? You can change parameters and say "Go ahead and try it. No one's getting hurt, it's a computer game." They love it because they can understand what I am talking about and comprehend the information much better.

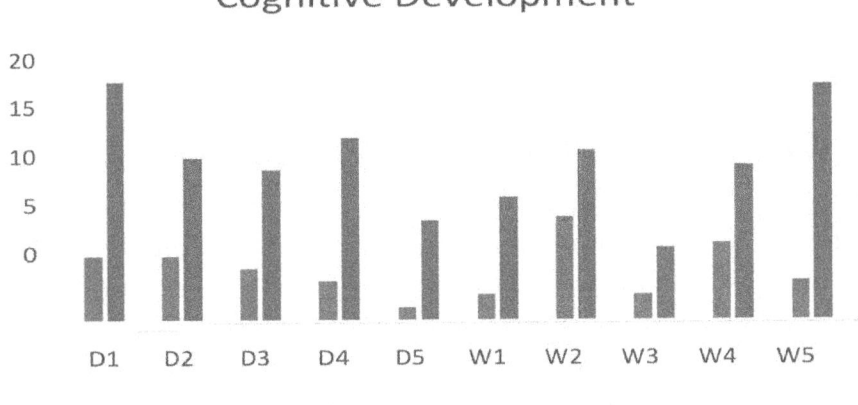

Figure 1 - Frequency of responses and coverage percentages to cognitive development. References are the number of times participants spoke of or referenced cognitive development. Coverages are frequency percentages for the invariant constituents.

W4 maintained,

"I think it's very important. You will be at the hallmark of being an educated person. You need to speak well and adequately. You need to write well. You need to be able to engage in a professional matter and express your opinion, your views, your diagnosis. Whatever it is. It's very important." W4 also stated, "As a mentor, if you notice people who just aren't quite cutting the mark, then you really have to step in and intervene, and advise those people to the best of your ability." W5 added, "Well, I would say cognitive development in a mentor/mentee relationship is moderately important. I would say because that is not really the goal of a mentor. That is not what its about. I think its more of support, emotional support and just guidance and following up or understanding the process going through a dissertation.

Theme 2 – Matching Process

Eight of the ten participants stated there were some sort of matching process between doctoral mentors and doctoral students. Seven of the ten participants also concluded student compatibility was involved in the matching process at the university at which they mentor. For example, D1 from one case stated,

> It's done a couple different ways. In that manner, we have some that are based upon what the topics of discussion may be. In other words, "The dissertation, I'm going to be thinking about doing this area or this area" and they might match somebody that has that professional experience. Other times, its kind of an open idea where there's a list and folks can go through that list and pick somebody who they think fits their study. The third way might be that somebody just, "Well, I know this person" and do that. Do I think it could be a little bit more formalized in how this university does things? Probably, but the ones I have had it's been, for the most part, pretty effective. A couple maybe not so, but for the most part, yes.

D3 maintained,

> "I think it's pretty good. My program director, she ... last year ... for instance, the most recent time they matched students last October, November. She brought a couple of us in. The instructor who had them for their very first class was in the room. She, as the program director, was there, and myself who have been a field advisor

longer than anyone at the program. The three of us in
the room, she went through the list with the instructor
who had them as their very first professor and got his
feedback, because he knows all the field advisors. He
also knew the students, because he spent seven weeks
with them. She was very concerned about proper
matching and looking at, again, organizational
leadership students come from very different
background, and making sure that people were aligned
with the right field advisor on a couple of different
dimensions. Things relative to personality, as well as
geographic closeness, as well as professional
background. I think the process where I am in my
program is very personal and very deliberate. Some
places, it may be as simple as throwing names in the
hat, I don't know, but we couldn't be further from that."

D4 stated,

"I'm fine with it. Our students can choose who they
want. They go through their classes and then they start
the process of building their committee, and starting to
think about, who do you want for your committee. Our
university is a little different. They are not given a
mentor at the very beginning of the program. They are
not really given a mentor, per se, until they are getting a
little closer to their dissertation process. I am at two
universities, and neither one is … well, the other one is
a little different. The other one is given a mentor kind of
at the beginning through their field experience process,
because they have to have some field experiences. I
have 12 students that I mentor at the other university
through their field experience process, and I become a

mentor almost for the program, even though I am only field experience. Does that make sense? It gives them a point of reference. They will ask me questions about things that have nothing to do with the field experience process. I think every university does it different. Sometimes you are given a mentor at the beginning, sometimes you do not get the mentor until towards the end. It just depends on the university structure."

From the second case, W1 stated,

Currently, I have good feelings about it, because they match based on the methodology style, so quantitative versus qualitative. Before it was not that kind of a thing. I think its great. They do not tell us ahead of time, like, 'Okay, we're going to be assigning you so and so, who's coming out of the retreat that they were just in.' All they do is just put it on our work schedule. We get assigned to them and then we meet them via phone and e-mail. They match our methodology expertise. "This is kind of funny. The chairs of the three different majors, the three different tracks, assign mentors or assign field advisors to the students. Some of them know their students and they know who would be a good fit with who. Some of them do not. Its a coin toss. I am not too sure I like that idea, but I'm not in a position to say anything. If I could have influence over that, I would ask the three chairs to talk to the people who teach the first three courses.

When asked how the university ensured compatibility during the matching process D3, from one case, stated,

They bring people into the room who know the students, because they have already taught them at one class, and who also know the people who are field advisors. Having people in the room who know everyone who is at the party to help do the matching. I think that is been effective. Its been a key plus. They are also very open too. If a match does not work, a match doesn't work. I think they ensure compatibility by letting the students choose their own team that supports them. They go through classes and they get to know people, get to know professors and support structures that they have in place in their classes. They talk to each other to get, who do you like, who don't you like, who would be good, who's interested, that kind of thing. The other thing that the one university that I am at does is, they have almost a dissertation portal type thing, where all of the available chair and readers for a dissertation committee are listed, with all of their research interests. Students can go to that portal, and they can go down and they can see our picture, and our experience, and then they can see our areas of interest.

From the other case, W3 stated,

It is mostly random, but I will tell you this. Let me tell you what usually happens, in my situation. I will teach a course, and it is usually a pretty pleasant experience. Doctoral students will say, "Well, Dr. Hoffer, do you do internship advising?" I say, "Yes." "Would you be my advisor for internship?" I say, "Yes. I can do that. You know, I have done that. I have done a lot of those, I can do that. I have time to do that for you. They just look for similarities in a research topic.

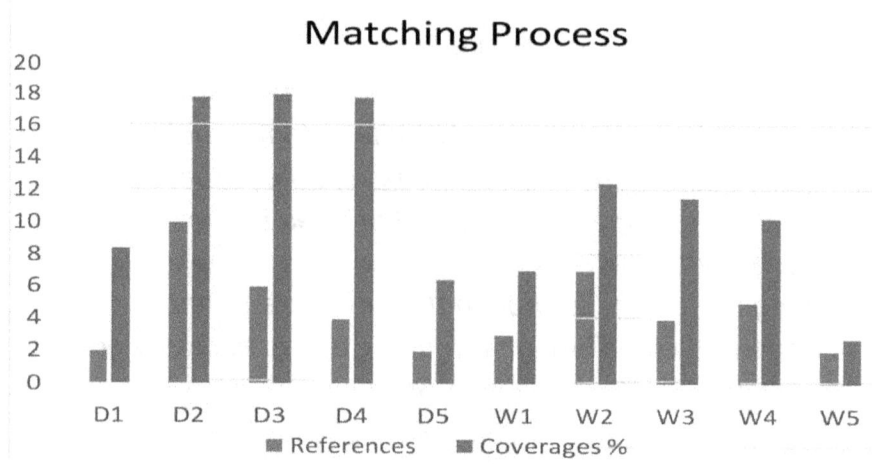

Figure 2 - Frequency of responses and coverage percentages to matching process. References are the number of times participants spoke of or referenced matching process. Coverages are frequency percentages for the invariant constituents.

Theme 3 – Indicators and Factors

All participants from both cases discussed important indicators and factors associated with building an effective mentoring relationship during the initiation phase of the relationship. D1, from one case, stated, "I think the trust to be able to have an open, honest discussion. I think also its important ... the mentor not be afraid to have those courageous conversations."

D2 maintained,

> I think free flow of communication, open communication. Again, I talked about being able to listen to them, listening skills and communications skills. Being able to paraphrase and summarize what they are saying to me so they feel heard and also to

help them to clarify their own goals or what they want to achieve. Establishing things like confidentiality. I think that is really important that what we talk about would stay with us, except for the kinds of things I would need to share with their program. I think getting to understand everyone's unique story. Meaning, I want them to know why I do this and my background. I want to learn their story. I do not think that you can mentor someone or be mentored by someone if you do not know who the other person really is and what drives them. That's key. Getting down to that level of understanding of each other. I think you need to be available. I am very careful about how many students I take on so that I can be fully available to the ones that I have committed to. I think sometimes mentors take on too many. Sometimes I think that is their desire to mentor students and sometimes I think its their desire to get whatever compensation comes along with that.

W1 from the second case stated,

Being available. Responding to the initial e- mail, they get an e-mail from the school saying, "Here's your new mentor's name. Here's your mentor's e-mail. Reach out to them." They usually do not reach out, so I reach out first trying to be proactive. Their return e-mail is one of the factors that helps develop the relationship. W2 also stated. "Making the student feel at ease talking to me. They do not know me, I am a stranger to them. They are being hit with a lot of different personalities very early in the program, a lot of expectations, a lot of demands and there is a lot of things that are vague and they do not know because they haven't experienced yet. I think one of the key factors, is an orientation to the process you are about to begin. In other words, a lot of people start a doctoral program, and have no idea what they are going to experience in the next three, or four, years, or five, or six, years. I ask good questions, and lay the ground work of expectations. In other words, I let students know that there are going to be changes in their lives. I think being welcoming. Telling the person when they leave the initial interview we can have a meeting or two, that they are always welcome to call, email, or come back to the office for an appointment.

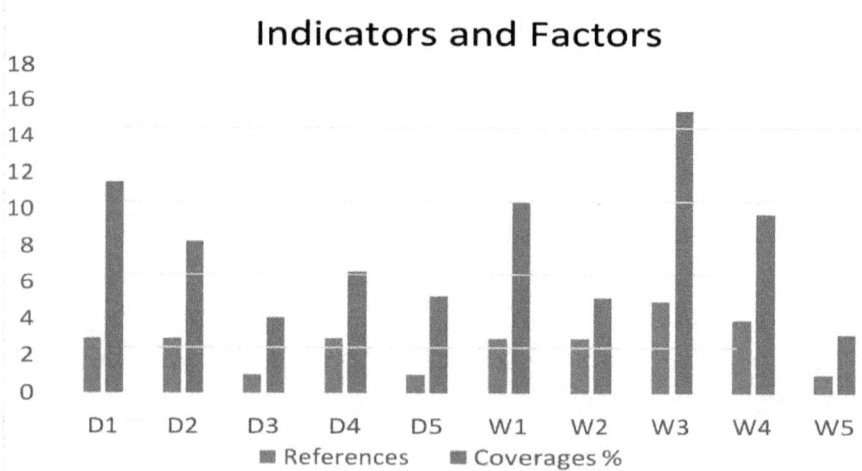

Figure 3 - Frequency of responses and coverage percentages to indicators and factors. References are the number of times participants spoke of or referenced indicators and factors. Coverages are frequency percentages for the invariant constituents.

Theme 4 – Influence

Participants from both cases described how their influence on doctoral students could have an effect on the doctoral students' cognitive development. D1 stated,

> I think its humongous. Its huge because its contagious. The attitude is contagious. If we are guiding folks towards their process and that learning process and you are enthusiastic about the learning, enthused about working with somebody so that they learn, its contagious. That is going to carry over with them too, so I think it's vitally important."

D3 maintained,

> I think its essential. I believe very strongly in positive reinforcement. Its tough when you have someone who might need a little tough love or a push. How do you temper that and how do you deliver that message? That is difficult. I think that its very important that if someone needs guidance and help; how you deliver that message is very important, because I can really make or break someone's determination to continue [on]. I think that is a very delicate process that you can not take too lightly. I encourage my students on a regular basis that they can do this. The cognitive and the emotional is so closely related in the doctoral process. If they are emotionally feeling frustrated, or like they can't do it, mentally they're thinking, "I can't do it," that becomes a cognitive process too.

W1 from the second case included,

I believe everybody loves praise and encouragement, so my influence is definitely going to affect their cognitive development if they apply themselves. If I do notice that the next draft has changes implemented that I suggested, I will point it out, like, "Thank you, this is great. This looks fantastic. Well done with your revisions." They usually seem to feel good about that, because the returned e-mail is usually a, "Thank you, I was worried," or "Phew, glad I did that right." It sounds like, to me, that they are trying to please me. I just want to make sure that they do get the props that they deserve.

W3 maintained,

Well, if an instructor is positive, and proactive, and informative, it allows the student to gain confidence. I think if you lay out the information, and then the students can internalize what it is that needs to be done." W4 insist, *"I think keeping up on the research yourself. Keeping involved professionally, living by example. I think once your students know that you are a writer, a researcher, a reader, a presenter, a committee member. Once they know that you can handle [all of] those layers, multiple layers of your life as a professional, and discuss that with them in a very collegiate way, I think that really helps the mentor relationship between the mentor and the mentee. Both individually, and in group. If things are discussed in class.*

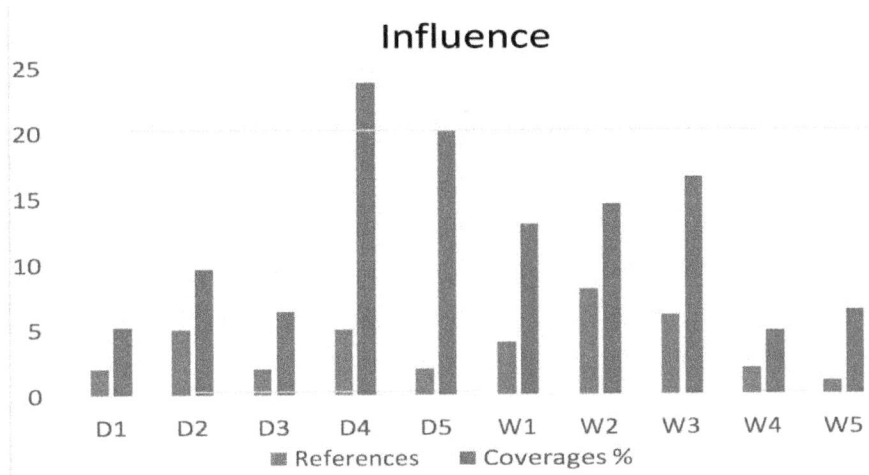

Figure 4 - Frequency of responses and coverage percentages to influence. References are the number of times participants spoke of or referenced influence. Coverages are frequency percentages for the invariant constituents.

Theme 5 – Student Networking

Student networking was a topic of discussion when all participants talked about the matching process and how the university ensures student compatibility. Participants felt students networked with each other to see who had the best mentor or who had a mentor that was very helpful to a doctoral student's needs. D1 from one case stated,

> *I do see student networking a lot. Just like I said. They are looking at trying to get likes and compatible mentors or at least backgrounds that match up so you're not having somebody you do not want to be paired up with.*

D3 maintained,

Absolutely; student networking happens. My very first year of doing this in 2010, I started with three advisees and then I ended up with seven, because four students jumped ship from the same advisor to me. I can only assume that once the first one did, the other three were like, "We're right behind you." I can only assume that. Yes, they will question it. They talk amongst themselves.

D5 also insisted, "Yes, and the students seek out mentors in addition to the college leadership matching mentors with mentees. Some of it is word-of-mouth too. I've gotten a lot of people from student referrals."

From the second case, W1 stated,

In many cases, they, the students, end up asking around, other learners, and then they try to get with that person that people suggest. Sometimes its the best case for these students because of others success. They try to find a good fit for what they are looking for.

W3 maintained,

Oh, yes, yes. The student networking part is huge. It should be that way. There are instructors, that students say, "Well, you have got to stay away from this person … Everybody has an agenda. Yes. I think the doctoral process does allow for some of that to take place, over a period. Having courses, networking with students, each other. Getting to know people. Putting people on a list. Keeping them off a list. That all happens. Professors know that, and students know that. I like that, because I tend to do well. I have good rapport with my students. I am transparent. When students see how I operate they tend to tell others and that is how I end up with many students as my mentees.

W4 also stated,

But as I said, if it did not work out, if you and I really clashed for example, you could say, "The heck with Dr. A. I'm going to put in for somebody else." Usually students did that by talking with each other. Its like advertising, your best advertisement is word of mouth. They would say, "This person is never there in the office, they don't get back to me, I didn't like the way he spoke to me. I requested a change, and I got Person B, and that person has been really satisfactory." Many times that will happen, and somebody else will also request Person B.

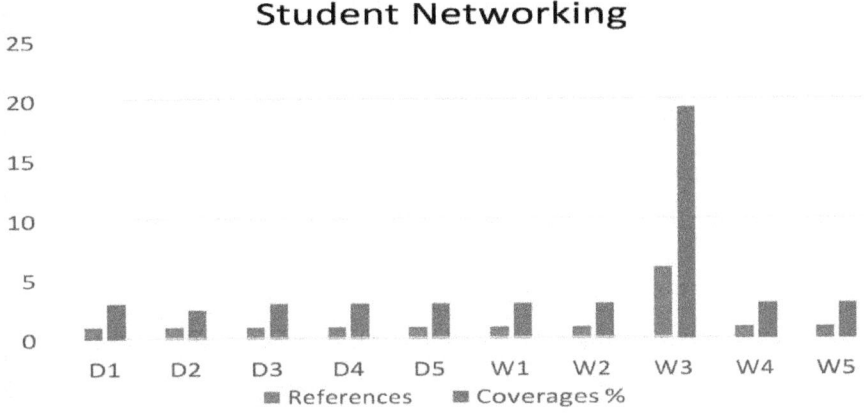

Figure 5 - Frequency of responses and coverage percentages to student networking. References are the number of times participants spoke of or referenced student networking. Coverages are frequency percentages for the invariant constituents.

Theme 6 – Role

Doctoral mentors perceive their role as a mentor in different ways. All participants expressed the importance of being a doctoral mentor. For example, D1 stated,

> *I think the role of being a mentor is extremely important, especially when you talk about leadership development. We can get institutional education, but actually focusing on an individual level of helping somebody and guiding them towards what their values are, core values, what our mission is, and what our vision is going to be. I think that is critical for that mentor to help that person and deal with their individual trials and tribulations of the peaks and the moments that they're doing well.*

D2 maintained,

> *I would help them with goal setting, much of which was structured by their program, different areas where they had to develop competency or demonstrate competency. I would brainstorm with them about goal setting in these various areas and what kinds of aspects of their work would satisfy the competencies in these different areas.*

D3 stated,

> *Its trying to be a resource, whether I can answer questions, having been through the program before them, or being involved in the program now, or at least helping facilitate. I remember what was like to be that person and to have questions and not necessarily know*

who might have the answer. While I may not have the answer, I can at least generally direct them to who may have the answer. I think that the role there is just a resource.

D4 added,

I think that students are very intimidated by the dissertation process specifically, and so I really try to encourage them that they can do it. Because its quite overwhelming. I try to break the process down as much as I can so that they can look at it in smaller pieces instead of the overall picture, because the overall picture may be overwhelming. I try to be a cheerleader for them, really encourage them, and set deadlines. I also try to be a support structure for them personally. Life continues to happen while you are writing your doctorate, or you are writing your dissertation, or you're going through your doctoral program, so I really encourage them not to quit, and to keep going.

W1, from another case stated.

I would describe my role as a mentor as more of a guide. I want the doctoral learner to do as much of the work on their own as they can. I have noticed, as the years have gone by, that learners have begun to rely on me as a mentor to help them figure out how to do their doctoral dissertation, and that's not my role. They turned it into, kind of like, a classroom, and part of that is the institution's fault, because they started putting these elements in the classroom. They want correction, and they want editing for free, and that kind of thing.

Recently, I would say, more of a guide that sticks to what the rules are for completing their dissertation.

W2 goes in-depth and maintained,

Right now, I am a mentor with doctoral students as they do their internship. At this university, in the doctoral program, all the students go through the whole program from the beginning to the end as a cohort. They build relationships with one another. During their second course in the program, they are assigned a field advisor, and that's what I am, a field advisor. We meet with our new students and we explain what the internship is as part of our accreditation. We talk to the students, we explain to them what is expected of them. We have three internship courses for the education leadership majors. The organizational and higher Education leadership majors have two internship courses. The first one is at the sixth course in their program of studies so its the end of the summer of their first year.

W4 stated,

I perceive it as something that is very important. A very small percentage of the American population has their doctorate, and I think that is the way it should be. We do not want to just be taking people into the program because they think its something to do, maybe just a lofty goal. But really, people who have the tenacity and the intelligence, and attribute their own effort to success. All of the things you look for in somebody who really should be recognized eventually as an academic, and an intellectual." W5 maintained, "A mentor should be available, as available as possible for the student because they're leaning on you."

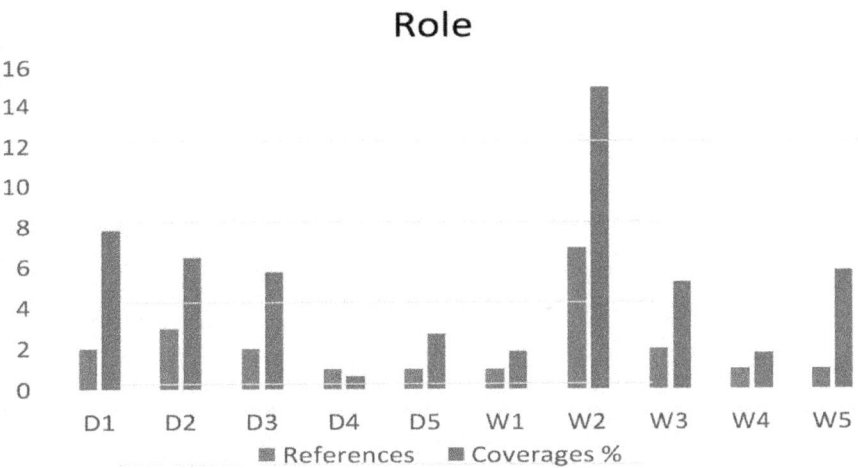

Figure 6 - Frequency of responses and coverage percentages to role. References are the number of times participants spoke of or referenced role. Coverages are frequency percentages for the invariant constituents.

Theme 7 – Relationships

Relationships played a significant role in the mentor/mentee relationship establishment. Three interview questions touched on mentoring relationships in doctoral programs. All participants expressed the importance and specific indicators of building an effective mentoring relationship for student success. D1, from one case explained,

> "I think that trust factor is there, right? If you wanted somebody to really trust you, you got to have that credibility. You got to have the knowledge, and obviously the credentials, to back up the fact that you

are mentoring somebody on that level, and you have to have that trust factor. I think also its important that the mentor not be afraid to have those courageous conversations. What I mean by that is, actually telling people the way it is, that if somebody's not doing a good job, that you're explaining to them that, "Hey, you're not doing a good job and this is why."

D2 maintained,

I think its very important to establish trust and rapport initially to demonstrate that I'm a good listener. I would listen to what their issues are, their needs are [first of all]. Then talk about how I could be helpful to them. Ways that I could be helpful based on their needs, based on what I felt I had to offer in my experience. I would identify strengths in areas where they could improve or get stronger." D3 stated, "I think that early meeting where you establish that I'm going to meet with you one-on-one; we're going to have a conversation. Its going to allow us to develop hopefully a rapport versus me in front of a room of even just three people.

D4 stated, "I think you need to be available. I'm very careful about how many students I take on so … I can be fully available to the ones … I have committed to." D5 explained, "It's very important to build the trust in the beginning. It normally starts with the observation and providing critical feedback in a way of being supportive. The trust factor is very important at the initial engagement of mentoring."

From the second case, W1 stated,

Being available is very important when building a relationship. Responding to initial e-mails and being able to communicate effectively." W2 maintained, *"First [of all], is making the student feel at ease talking to me. They do not know me, I am a stranger to them. They are being hit with a lot of different personalities very early in the program. A lot of expectations, a lot of demands and there is a lot of things that are vague and they do not know, because they haven't experienced yet, so making students feel comfortable is critical.*

W3 also stated,

Building a relationship is a process. It starts out low and slow, and builds over [a period of] time. If you have two wrong people working early, they can work as long, and as hard, as they want to build a relationship, and it will never happen.

W5 added, "Responses, so in other words, if there's an email trail or a phone conversation occurring regularly, that's a pretty strong indicator in the forefront that a good relationship is going to last."

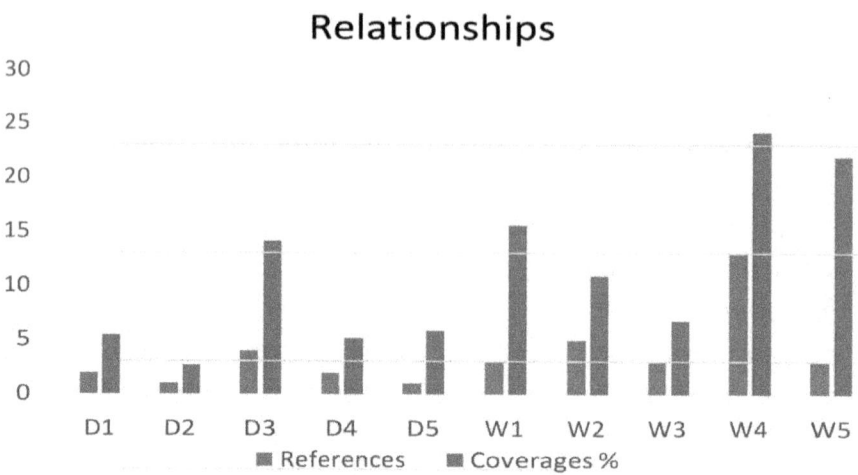

Figure 7 - Frequency of responses and coverage percentages to relationships. References are the number of times participants spoke of or referenced relationships. Coverages are frequency percentages for the invariant constituents.

Theme 8 – Perceptions

All participants provided their perceptions on the mentoring relationship and student compatibility in doctoral programs. Perceptions of participants were from personal experiences being a mentor to doctoral students. For example, D2 explained, "I found some students needed a lot of handholding and others needed less, and some try to do stuff without talking to me. Sometimes they would get in trouble because they would register for the wrong courses and such." D3 stated,

> *Usually, when a student reaches out to me because they have questions or they need to just talk, generally speaking, they need to do it sooner than later. I try to make myself available to do that. I am very open with giving out. Like I said, my mobile number, and I am*

responsive I think more than most colleagues that I have.

Participant D4 maintained,

Doctoral students come in sometimes with the same attitude that they've had in their lower levels of education where, "If I work hard I get an A, and if I don't get an A then I'll argue with the professor until I can get that A. Or I'll do extra stuff until I can get that A." Doctoral professors are a little different. Its a little bit of a different level of education. They are like, "No, you can't turn it in again, you can't do it over." You are not going to get all A's necessarily, and that's an okay thing. Getting a doctorate is hard. I think changing that mindset of, you need to be okay with working hard and doing your best and focusing more on the learning process than the outcome, within reason.

W1, from the second case perceived a mentoring relationship as doctoral students owning their doctoral journey. W1 explained, "In an idealist world, I want to say that these are doctoral learners, they have the mental maturity to understand that they need to be able to exceed without necessarily having praise on every single good thing that they do." W3 stated,

I have created two doctoral programs, from scratch. A Ph.D., and an Ed.D. for a university in … Maryland. I was a director of doctoral studies for 12 years. I brought 400 candidates into the two programs. Monitored them. That would be teaching the courses, monitoring all their internships. I was the internship monitor for [all of] those people. Then, I served on all doctoral committees for quality control, because it was a new program. Currently, I teach doctoral level courses. I have a lot of experience mentoring doctoral students; the majority of it has been very rewarding.

W4 maintained,

The mentoring relationship is very important and I have seen where there were great mentoring experiences, good mentoring experiences, and bad mentoring experiences. I have seen where the majority of mentors and mentees that have a trusting relationship succeed over those that do not. I also believe if you are not a reflective person before you become a mentor you probably don't need to be a mentor.

W5 stated,

The early stage of building a mentoring relationship is very important. Understanding how compatible a mentor and mentee is beneficial to the relationship and helps the student effectively make it through their program. Building the relationship is like a two-way street. There has to be some give and take on both parts, and there has to be some sort of meeting in the middle. When it is only a one-way street and there is no give my [sic] one particular person, the relationship will be ruined and the student may end up dropping out of the doctoral program.

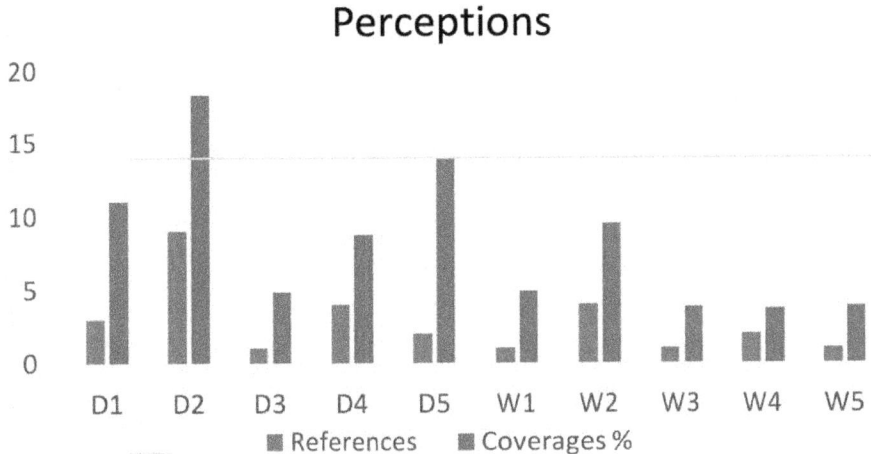

Figure 8 - Frequency of responses and coverage percentages to perceptions. References are the number of times participants spoke of or referenced perceptions. Coverages are frequency percentages for the invariant constituents.

Theme 9 – Improvements

Doctoral mentors explained different ways where building an effective mentoring relationship can improve along with ensuring student compatibility. From the first case, D1 explained,

> *From an individual perspective, I think you need to have people that engage that want to be mentors for the right reason, so maybe a screening process. To look at that and say, "Hey, why you want to do this?" The other as far as the institutional approach, it might be a better match rather than just looking and them matching up, there's actually some kind of maybe formalized mechanism to do that. I do not know what that would look like off the top of my head, but maybe that might be a better way to do that. Maybe a drop-down option or something like that to see if there are similar*

interest." D2 indicated, "I think figuring out effective ways to match mentors and mentees in terms of their interests and aims. Also, I think there can be training and professional development for mentors.

D3 maintained, "I think that conscious planning and deliberate matching can be improved." D4 stated,

I think it would be better if universities gave a student a mentor at the beginning of their program, as opposed to waiting until a few classes go by. I also believe mentors should touch basis with their mentees at least once a month to keep that support structure intact.

D5 also stated, "Having more structured programming at the collegiate level between professors and learners."

From the second case, W1 explained, "It seems like we do not have enough power to approve things at the mentor stage, because everything has to go through committee and then the school. I think things would improve if we had more power."

W2 stated,

A couple of the things that I would do is have field advisors introduced during the first course. Have the field advisors talk to the whole class together. This is what is expected. This is what we will do for you, this is what we expect of you, but they do not.

W3 maintained,

Probably, orientation. Maybe, an orientation, or help me say this. An orientation experience, where there would be eight, or 10, faculty members, and doctoral mentors to say this is what I do or this is what I used to do. Maybe sell themselves to students.

W4 stated,

Probably a couple of things. One would be for those who mentor to discuss what that relationship should look like. What is it that the university wants to get across in terms of their mentoring program? There needs to be some [kind of] philosophical, or mission statement, about what they ... meaning the collective professors that do that mentoring ... as well as the deans or whoever is above them, what they would like to see as the hallmark of their mentoring program. Two, I think student feedback is important too. There are always questionnaires or surveys, things like that, that can be done. You can ask lots of questions about the logistics, as well as the quality of what they see when they are being mentored. It should help inform the people that do the mentoring, the university, and let the students know that their voices are heard.

W5 added, "I think mentoring relationships should not be matched through third party. I think that is less effective."

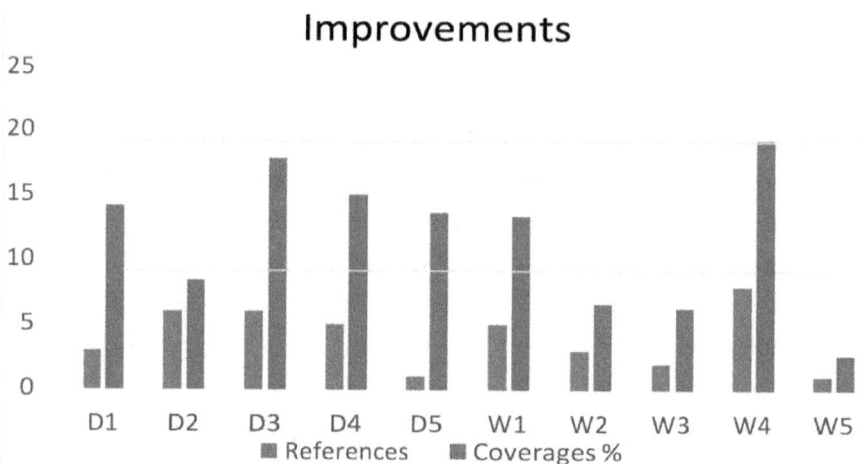

Figure 9 - Frequency of responses and coverage percentages to improvements. References are the number of times participants spoke of or referenced improvements. Coverages are frequency percentages for the invariant constituents.

Summary

Chapter 4 contained the findings and results describing and interpreting the perceptions of doctoral mentors on mentoring relationships and student compatibility in doctoral programs. The main goal of the study was to examine the gap of research and literature to understand this studies' specific problem, which is high attrition rates of doctoral students that may be attributed to mentor/mentee relationships. The study examined the perceptions of 10 doctoral mentors from two universities in the state of Delaware. Using a multiple-case study supported efforts to collect data, transcribe the data, and interpret the data into emerging themes and patterns (Yin, 2014).

Chapter 5 contained the nine core themes that emerged from the data analysis process and interpretation of the data contained in Chapter 4. A rich and thick description of these core themes came from 10 participant statements from

11 interview questions. Chapter 5 included the study findings, limitations of the study, implications, recommendations for leadership and future research, and conclusions.

Chapter 5

Conclusions and Recommendations

The purpose of this exploratory, multiple-case study was to explore doctoral mentors' perceptions on mentoring relationship experiences and student compatibility in doctoral programs. Through a purposeful selection process, selected participants for the study contributed their experiences and perceptions on mentoring relationships and student compatibility in doctoral programs. This qualitative multiple-case study was the approach for exploring the perceptions of 10 doctoral mentors from two universities in the state of Delaware. The participants' responses to open-ended questions pertaining to the study were collected using a voice tape-recorder which was transcribed into a word document and entered in NVivo 11 for data analysis.

Chapter 4 includes the explanation of the study findings. Chapter 5 contains discussion of the results of the multiple-case study. The limitation and implications for leaders are also presented, followed by recommendations for leadership. The chapter also includes recommendations for future research and ends with a conclusion.

Findings

Based on the results from the data analysis, nine themes introduced in Chapter 4 were presented relating to the main research question and research sub-questions:

- R1: How do doctoral mentors perceive the role of student mentoring and student compatibility in doctoral programs?

- S1: How do doctoral mentors perceive the importance of the initiation phase of a mentor/mentee relationship?

- S2: How do doctoral mentors perceive the importance of mentee cognitive development during the mentor/mentee relationship?

The focus of the study was to identify themes and patterns associated with mentoring relationships. Eleven open-ended interview questions were prepared as the primary instrument for study participants to provide answers to. Ten doctoral mentors reflected and gave their experiences and perceptions on mentoring relationships and student compatibility in doctoral programs at two universities in the state of Delaware.

The nine emergent themes revealed in Chapter 4 were:

1. Cognitive Development
2. Matching Process
3. Indicators and Factors
4. Influence
5. Student Networking
6. Role
7. Relationships
8. Perceptions
9. Improvements

Theme 1. Cognitive Development

Each participant discussed the importance of cognitive development as it pertained to doctoral students' ability to research and writing the dissertation. The reviewed literature stated cognitive development as a mental process that results in the maturation of various experiences a doctoral student will face (McLeod, 2015). Each participant understood the need to assist mentees to develop a strong understanding of the doctoral process to successfully complete the dissertation. Participants also understood it was the student's responsibility to learn how to adapt to changes and learn new ways of researching. Participants suggest implementation of strategies where students can self- regulate thought and learning processes (Hezlett, 2005). A literature review implicated the success and retention of doctoral students requires cognitive interest to expand inquiry and seek knowledge (Francois, 2014).

Theme 2. Matching Process

Doctoral mentors had a difference of opinion pertaining to the matching process currently being used at their perspective university. In the first case 20% of participants were not in favor of the matching process, 20% did not know there was a matching process in place, and 60% were in favor of how the matching process was done.

Compatibility was also a concern where participants felt the need for academic institutions to incorporate more effective ways to match mentors to mentees. Reviewed literature stated the importance of academic institutions matching mentors with mentees that share the same similar qualities (Wang & Fulton, 2012). The academic institution's primary focus is to establish an effective and successful mentoring process (Glanville & Porche, 2000).

Theme 3. Indicators and Factors

Participants highlighted different indicators and factors associated with building an effective mentoring relationship during the initiation phase of the relationship. Building trust with mentees was illustrated as being the main indicator when building an effective mentoring relationship. Mentees fanaticize about the support and trust level given by mentors during the initiation phase of the mentoring relationship (Kram, 1983). By overcoming difficult issues between mentors and mentees, a high level of trust must be built and considered essential for doctoral students successfully completing the doctoral program (Cowin et al., 2012).

Another indicator and factor concluded was the importance of establishing effective communication between mentors and mentees. Based on the reviewed literature, mentors and mentees ability to communicate was important when developing an interpersonal human relationship (Buzatu & Pipas, 2014). Poor communication can lead to distrust and inhibit doctoral students from completing the doctoral program (Yob & Crawford, 2012). Mentors and mentees must communicate what the expectations are and what goals need to be reached to maintain an effective relationship (Ricks, 2013).

Availability and clear expectations played a key role as an indicator and factor to building the relationship. A lack of available time presents challenges for mentors to assist mentees on doctoral journeys (Singh & Mahomed, 2013). Experienced mentors needed to invest quality time and commitment for developing an effective mentoring relationship

(Rekha & Ganesh, 2012). Psychological support provides students a level of comfort by addressing emotional and personal needs, and providing moral support to balance students' academic demands (Ligadu, 2012). Clear expectations in developing mentoring relationships are critical for mentors and mentees. Expectations can be concrete or generic, self-directed, or participative, and made clear through verbal communications or assumed (Huskins et al., 2011). Once expectations are clarified between mentors and mentees the relationship can begin by setting goals for mentees to meet at certain intervals until program completion (Evans & Laura, 2012).

Theme 4. Influence

Participants explained how personal influences can impact doctoral students' success and may inhibit or progress student's cognitive development throughout the doctoral process. Each participant expressed a desire to motivate and encourage mentees to ensure the mentee completes the doctoral program with support of the mentor. Doctoral mentors acknowledged mentees need to be encouraged while going through the doctoral program. Mentors also acknowledged encouragement and support levels needed by each doctoral student will vary from one student to the next. Mentoring support and encouragement should be developed to meet the needs of each student while students receive continuous feedback from mentors (Utrilla & Grande, 2012). Mentors sustain the ability to empower mentees into performing at a level consistent with the institutions' academic norms (Sugimoto, 2012b).

Mentors noted personal negative influences may negatively impact a mentee's desire to complete the doctoral degree. According to Kram (1983), all mentees believe mentors are to support and guide them through the doctoral process. Doctoral mentors from both cases explained the seriousness of a mentor's lack of positive influence has on mentees. While the participants addressed the negative impact on mentees from a lack of positive influence from mentors, all were concerned about the institution enforcing a productive mentoring process. According to Sarri (2011), time and effort are necessary for academic institutions to process and incorporate an effective mentoring process, but worth it.

Theme 5. Student Networking

Doctoral mentors suggested student networking successful as a means for mentees to acquire an effective mentor. While some participants perceived the matching process working well at their perspective university, some saw the need for change. Many of the participants noted an increasing number of mentees finding mentors through peer networking. According to Vekkaila, mentors influence doctoral students, but students are also influenced by peers (Vekkaila et al., 2014). Doctoral mentors also noted student networking is a normal cultural influence. According to Blickle et al (2010), cultural aspects that pertain to mentoring relationships were essential to facing challenges while trying to be successful. Reviewed literature stated culture in which institutions are accustomed to when matching mentors and mentees may inadvertently change because students seek out each other to find mentors (Tagreed, 2012). Mentees seek out assistance from peers because of a perceived cultural difference between mentors and mentees (Merriweather & Morgan, 2013).

Theme 6. Role

Doctoral mentors highlighted the importance of playing a positive role in the doctoral student's journey to complete the doctoral program. According to the reviewed literature, mentors play pivotal roles to help mentees reach specific goals and help students to work at full potential (Lundgren & Orsillo, 2012). Mentors noted they should be able to provide guidance to mentees through personal experiences and skills acquired (Evans & Forbes, 2012). Doctoral mentors also noted their role as a mentor is to assist mentees with setting academic goals. A mentee's self-efficacy is important pertaining to goal setting. According to reviewed literature, human behavior is greatly stimulated in a variety of ways, and one-way behavior is greatly stimulated by self-influence is by self- efficacy (Bandura, 1986).

Several doctoral mentors noted their role of mentoring pertained to being a guide and being available to show support when support is needed. One of the mentoring functions highlighted by doctoral mentors is psychosocial support during the mentoring relationship (Chun et al., 2012). Mentors noted they should provide advice, guidance, and support throughout the whole doctoral process (Yob & Crawford, 2012). The emotional support mentors provide to mentees strengthens the mentoring relationship (Sanfey et al., 2013).

Theme 7. Relationships

Doctoral mentors noted mentoring relationships are developed from the initial meeting of mentors and mentees where mentors assist mentees in their quest to complete their doctoral degree (Kram 1983). The literature review discussed various mentoring functions provided by mentors through (a) career support, (b) psychosocial support, and (c) role modeling (Chun et al., 2012). Mentors posited indicators and factors of building an effective mentoring relationship with communication being important when building mentoring relationships. Communication can have a negative or positive effect on relationships; a line of open communication is important for mentors and mentees (Fischer, 2013).

Mentors also noted trust must be the main factor to build a strong relationship. To help mentees reach academic goals, mentors are taught how to build trust which is a positive characteristic for mentors (Rekha & Ganesh, 2012). Literature reviewed stated to overcome difficult situations in the mentoring relationship, building a high level of trust is essential meeting the demands of students completing doctoral programs (Cowin et al., 2012). Mentors stated building trust is being available to the mentee when assistance is needed. Doctoral mentors noted they must be available to mentees when needed, which is part of setting the initial expectations of the mentoring relationship.
Mentors also stated having responsive attitudes tend to build stronger mentoring relationships (Dreyer, 2014).

Theme 8. Perceptions

All participants provided their perceptions on mentoring experiences and student compatibility. Overall, each doctoral mentor enjoys the experience of helping mentees achieve goals and reach graduation. Mentors understood all mentees are different and have different attributes that distinguish them from other mentees. Mentors also highlighted mentees experience easy transition to work more independently on the research project when a sense of self-confidence exists. The first mentoring model discussed in the literature review was the separation phase where mentees may feel confident enough to separate from mentors to complete goals and objectives (Khosla, 2013).

Some mentors expressed new doctoral students may come with the same attitude experienced in lower-level education. Some students have unexpected expectations of what doctoral classes will be like and expect to get an 'A' in every class. Mentors explained the student's motivation is more on getting an 'A' instead of focusing on the research project. Mentors have addressed to students that unexpected expectations can lead to unwarranted challenges for doctoral students pursuing a doctoral degree. Reviewed literature stated the starting point of the mentor/mentee relationship is when expectations should be clarified and understood by both (Kram, 1983). Expectations can be formal or informal, as long as a mutual agreement coalesces between the mentor and mentee (Huskins et al., 2011).

Theme 9. Improvements

Doctoral mentors in this study addressed the need to improve the mentoring process at each respective university. Each mentor noted mentoring relationships are not easy to establish and includes a time and commitment for academic institutions and mentors. Mentoring initiatives require proper planning to develop and achieve mentor relationship success (Stephens, Doherty, Bennett, & Margey, 2014). Mentors highlighted the need for mentors to be assigned to mentees at the very beginning of the doctoral program. In the reviewed literature, Kram (1983) explained the importance of early initiation of mentoring stating the early initiation phase is where clear expectations are clarified to begin the relationship process.

Several doctoral mentors noted the need to have a more conscious plan trying to meet the needs of mentors and mentees. Mentors highlighted the need of having a clear understanding of the objectives and measurements of the objectives of the mentoring process (Kiran et al., 2012). Mentors noted conscious planning and deliberate matching of mentors and mentees would improve a working relationship. Mentors continuously noted academic institutions must be more organized and have structured programming. Literature reviewed stated, to address doctoral student attrition rates, academic institutions must pay close attention to and evaluate current mentoring policies set in place (Brill et al., 2014).

Other mentors reflected on the need to improve the matching of mentors and mentees. Participating doctoral mentors agreed for the need of an effective way to match mentors with mentees, whereas one of the mentors did not see a need to improve anything with the mentor/mentee process at the university. Most mentors noted there needs to be a process to figure out effective ways to match mentors and mentees in terms of their interests and aims. Some mentors stated there needs to be an effective orientation with mentors and mentees to successfully be paired together. Reviewed literature stated, many academic institutions develop mentoring programs to assist mentors and mentees in establishing a compatible relationship where the matching process is successful (Poronsky, 2012).

Limitations of the Study

The central limitation of this study involved the demographic characteristics. This research study was limited to a small number of research participants in a specific geographical area. The purposeful sampling may not be representative of the entire population of doctoral mentors in doctoral programs, limiting generalization by focusing on two universities in the state of Delaware. Qualitative research allowed for the exploration of doctoral mentor perceptions and interpret the perceptions to make meaning of the experiences (Townsend, Cox, & Li, 2010). However, this sample size did not reflect the entire population of doctoral mentors, which may be more represented and generalized through a quantitative study.

The sample participants in this research study consisted of six females and four male doctoral mentors. Gender was not a criterion for this study. The purposeful sample also lacked diversity and heavily favored Caucasians. The sample participants in this study consisted of eight Caucasians and two African-Americans. The absence of a diverse group resulted in the absence of other perceptions of mentoring relationships and student compatibility in doctoral programs. Ethnicity was not a criterion for this study.

Delimitations of the Study

There were several delimitations for this study. Only 10 doctoral mentors from two universities were selected for this study. The current study focused on investigating the perceptions of doctoral mentors in the state of Delaware. The second delimitation narrowed the selection of doctoral mentors who had mentoring experience for over three years. Another delimitation also narrowed the study to a specific geographical location. More specifically, a delimitation of selecting doctoral mentors from one small state rather than various sample sizes from larger states.

Implications

A multiple-case study design was appropriate for this exploratory study as the rationale that included the ability to access more information of doctoral mentors' perceptions on mentoring relationships and student compatibility in doctoral programs, which was the purpose of this study (Yin, 2014). Research from this multiple-case study produced nine themes from the perceptions of 10 participants and several observations. All data sources came from 10 doctoral mentors that comprised of two different cases.

The nine themes involved findings resolving one research question and two sub-questions. The data analysis produced examples of doctoral mentors' perception of their role on student mentoring and student compatibility in doctoral programs (R1). The data analysis also produced examples of doctoral mentors' perception on the importance of the initiation phase of a mentor/mentee relationship (S1) and doctoral mentors' perception on the importance of mentees' cognitive development during the mentor/mentee relationship (S2).

The findings section included significant highlighted statements and quotes from doctoral mentors' comments along with supporting literature. The implications are implied by the research data for consideration and discussion about the study and for implications to academic leadership. The nine core themes provided the highlighted and notable implications for interpretations from doctoral mentors' perceptions of the mentoring relationship and student compatibility:

1. The specific perceptions from participants were unique adding knowledge to the body of literature based on the most significant themes of matching process, indicators and factors, student networking, role, perceptions, and improvements.
2. The themes explained a definite need to reevaluate doctoral mentoring processes across academic institutions.
3. The themes explained a need to make improvements with mentor/mentee matching.

    The study results supported the purpose of the study and answered the research question and two sub-questions. The relationships between theme two (matching process), theme six (role), and theme eight (perceptions) aligned in understanding participants' perception on student mentoring and student compatibility. Participants perceived their role as a guide to mentees and being available to meet mentees' needs. Participants also indicated they assisted mentees with setting goals and objectives. Mentors are very instrumental in helping mentees plan and reach goals (Lundgren & Orsillo, 2012).

    Participants expressed a difference of opinions pertaining to the matching process and how it relates to student compatibility. Participants understand cultural difference may inhibit a mentee from attaining an effective relationship. Cultural differences tend to lead students to seek out other students for support in finding a mentor. Participants addressed the need to improve processes on making these cultural differences work when matching mentors and mentees.

    The initiation phase of the mentoring process seemed to be very important to effectively build a mentoring relationship. Every moment of the doctoral process is important to the doctoral student and having support from the beginning is critical. Once an effective mentoring relationship is established mentors understand the importance of building upon the mentees cognitive development. A mentee's cognitive development assists in the research and writing of the actual dissertation. The assessment of these implications aligned well with the research question and sub-questions. Academic institutions should examine, analyze, and review existing policies and procedures on doctoral mentoring procedures and make strategic plans on making necessary revisions (Kiran et al., 2012).

Implications to Leaders

The importance of this study to leadership was to examine high attrition rates in doctoral programs that may be attributed to mentor/mentee relationships. The importance of this study to leadership was also to examine doctoral mentors' perceptions on mentoring relationships and student compatibility in doctoral programs. The perceptions might be useful in the development of new mentoring policies and procedures at across all academic disciplines. Understanding why attrition exist may help to incorporate different mentoring programs to decrease attrition rates (Schmidt, Robinson, & Webster, 2014).

The implications within the findings of this study associated to mentoring relationships and student compatibility have limitless implications to leadership. The data may be appropriate to any academic institution employing novice doctoral mentors. Doctoral mentors represent one of the most important components to a doctoral student's success. The potential exists for academic leaders, provosts, and academic deans to use this information to create a formalized mentoring process that may contribute to decreasing attrition rates. This study substantiates the lack of consistent mentoring practices being used to establish effective relationships. This information may provide academic leaders information regarding the importance of matching mentors with mentees, the training of mentors, incorporating student input in the selection process, and consistently evaluating all mentoring policies and procedures to ensure its effectiveness.

Significance to Leadership

Mentoring relationships are important when developing a mentoring relationship in the doctoral program. Relationships formed by doctoral mentors and doctoral students are associated with a wide range of professional and academic success (Campbell et al., 2012). Academic leadership plays a major role for successfully establishing a mentoring relationship in doctoral programs (Campbell et al., 2012). The results of this study may provide information provosts, academic deans, and doctoral chairs can use to evaluate the mentoring process in doctoral programs. Institutional leaders may be able to provide improved or realigned mentorship practices addressing doctoral students learning needs, thus possibly increasing doctoral student completion rates. Understanding the dynamics and outcomes of this research study may help professional managers evaluate current mentoring policies and procedures to ensure placement of effective mentoring practices. Further, the results may provide academic leaders new insights for building effective mentorship relationships between doctoral mentors and doctoral mentees.

Recommendations for Leadership

The results of this research study may provide academic leadership better insight into the reasons doctoral students drop out. Academic leaders may also have a better insight on challenges mentoring relationships face pertaining to the matching process and student compatibility. Attrition rates are at 50% nationwide and leadership must focus on developing retention initiatives to decrease this trend (Di Pierro, 2012). Leadership strategies should include guidelines for training academic faculty selected to become doctoral mentors. The strategy could also include ways to incorporate student feedback on the mentoring process to understand what works and what does not work for them while pursuing their doctorate degree.

Academic leaders are encouraged to pay close attention to the findings of this research study to help evaluate current mentoring policies in place. Leadership should ensure each doctoral mentor knows and understands the academic institutions mentoring policy and procedures. One participant did not know the dynamics of their universities mentoring policy and that can be one too many. Leaders should look at indicators and factors associated with building an effective mentoring relationship provided in this research study. The research study may be used to facilitate initiatives to establish an effective mentor/mentee matching process. The results of this study show that some participants are not too involved in making changes or having a voice for change. Leadership could put together mentor forums where everyone can contribute to mentoring policy changes or revisions.

Recommendation for Future Research

The findings in this study provide insight and information regarding the exploration of doctoral mentors' perception on mentoring relationships experience and student compatibility. This study documented mentor's perceptions and mentoring experiences from two universities; however this study was limited to these two separate populations combined in the study and located in the state of Delaware. Further insight on mentoring relationships and student compatibility may be gained by conducting a qualitative multiple-study across more cases including more states. Conducting a research study on a larger population of doctoral mentors may be beneficial and influence major influencers and academic leaders across the globe.

A quantitative research study may also be beneficial to understand the number of doctoral students that dropout due to ineffective mentoring relationships. A quantitative study can also be used to understand the success rate of doctoral students that receive a mentor at the beginning of the doctoral program versus later in the program. Exploring data using quantitative research allows for numerical data to be examined for analysis through statistical referencing. A quantitative study will also generate new knowledge from the data. Further research should also investigate the challenges academic institutions face when trying to incorporate an effective mentoring process.

Conclusion

This multiple-case study aimed at exploring doctoral mentors' perceptions on mentoring relationship experiences and student compatibility in doctoral programs at two universities in the state of Delaware. The responses from the 10 doctoral mentors interviewed provided detailed discussion regarding their perceptions of mentoring relationship experiences and student compatibility. Participants of the study shared their experience and perceptions on mentoring relationships and student compatibility. Data was analyzed using NVivo 11 software. Nine major themes emerged through the data analysis. The nine themes were identified as (1) Cognitive Development, (2) Matching Process, (3) Indicators and Factors, (4) Influence, (5) Student Networking, (6) Role, (7), Relationships, (8) Perceptions, and (9) Improvements.

    Some participants indicated the need to improve in specific areas of the mentoring process to effectively mentor doctoral students. Implementing or having poor mentoring policies and procedure in place may negatively impact a mentee's relational experience with mentors (Brill & McCartney, 2008). The data also supported the need to have student involvement pertaining to developing a mentoring process. Student networking was a highly favorable topic of discussion to effectively match with a mentor. Many students look to their peers because of cultural differences a mentee may have with their mentor (Merriweather & Morgan, 2013).

    The main reason for this study was to add to current research and help improve mentoring relationships in doctoral programs across academia. This study was important because understanding perceptions of doctoral mentors regarding mentoring relationships and student compatibility in doctoral programs was timely and crucial for successful implementation of successful doctoral mentor/mentee matching processes. Additional research is required to determine the effects of mentees being assigned a mentor at the beginning of the doctoral program versus being assigned a mentor later in the doctoral program.

APPENDICES

Appendix A

Field Test Informed Consent Form

Informed Consent: Participants 18 Years of Age and Older

Dear (Name),

My name is Kenneth Jackson and I am a student at the University of Phoenix working on a Doctor of Management in Organizational Leadership degree. I am conducting a field test to test interview questions in connection with my research study entitled Exploring Perceptions of Mentor Relationships in Doctoral Programs. The purpose of this research study is to explore doctoral mentors' perception on mentoring relationship experiences and student compatibility in doctoral programs.

Participation would involve providing feedback on the interview questions for clarity, comprehension, and readability and provide any feedback on improvement. The researcher will make revisions, adjustments, or refinements to the interview questions that are of concern from any field test participant. The field test will take approximately 60 minutes to conduct.

Participation in for the field test is completely voluntary and you can withdraw from the field test at any time without any penalty or loss of benefits. The results of the research study maybe published but your identity will remain confidential and your name will not be made known to any outside party.

In this research, there are no foreseeable risks to you.

Although there may be no direct benefit to you, a possible benefit from your being part of this study is to improve ways to build successful mentoring relationships for doctoral programs.

If you have any questions about the field test, please call me at xxx-xxx-xxxx or e-mail at xxxxxxx@msn.com. For questions about your rights as a field test participant, or any concerns or complaints, please contact the University of Phoenix Institutional Review Board via email at IRB@phoenix.edu.

As a participant in this field test, you should understand the following:

1. You may decide not to be part of this study or you may want to withdraw from the field test before, during, or after information is collected. If you want to withdraw, you can do so without any problems by sending an e-mail to the researcher, stating you would like to withdraw from the research study. The e-mail address to send your withdrawal request is xxxxxxxxxxxxx@msn.com. Once received, the researcher will send a confirmation e-mail back and remove participant from the field test.
2. Your identity will be kept confidential.
3. The researcher, has fully explained the nature of the research study and has answered your questions and concerns.
4. If interviews are used, they may be recorded. If they are recorded, you must give permission for the researcher to record the interviews. You understand that the information from the recorded interviews may be transcribed. Data will be coded to assure that your identity is protected.
5. Data will be kept in a secure and locked area at (location) with single person access. After three years, the data collected will be shredded and incinerated.
6. The results of this study may be published.

By signing this form, you agree that you understand the nature of the study, the possible risks to you as a participant, and how your identity will be kept confidential. When you sign this form, this means that you are 18 years old or older and that you give your permission to volunteer as a participant in the study that is described here.

( ) I accept the above terms.

( ) I do not accept the above terms. (check one)

Signature of the field test participant

Date

Signature of the researcher
Date

Appendix B

Informed Consent Form

Informed Consent: Participants 18 Years of Age and Older

Dear (Name),

My name is Kenneth Jackson and I am a student at the University of Phoenix working on a Doctor of Management in Organizational Leadership degree. I am doing a research study entitled Exploring Perceptions of Mentor Relationships in Doctoral Programs. The purpose of the research study is to explore doctoral mentors' perceptions on mentoring relationship experiences and student compatibility in doctoral programs.

Participation would involve an interview process allowing you to answer open-ended questions in a one-to-one face-to-face setting. The interview will be tape-recorded to ensure correct dictation is transcribed. The interview process is expected to take approximately 60 minutes. Participation in the study is completely voluntary and you can withdraw from the study at any time without any penalty or loss of benefits. The results of the research study maybe published but your identity will remain confidential and your name will not be made known to any outside party.

In this research, there are no foreseeable risks to you.

Although there may be no direct benefit to you, a possible benefit from your being part of this study is to improve ways to build successful mentoring relationships for doctoral programs.

If you have any questions about the research study, please call me at xxx-xxx-xxxx or email me at: xxxxxx@msn.com. For questions about your rights as a study participant, or any concerns or complaints, please contact the University of Phoenix Institutional Review Board via email at IRB@phoenix.edu.

As a participant in this study, you should understand the following:

1. You may decide not to be part of this study or you may want to withdraw from the study at any time. If you want to withdraw, you can do so without any problems by sending an e-mail to the researcher, Kenneth Jackson, stating you would like to withdraw from the research study. The e-mail address to send your withdrawal request is xxxxxxxxxxxxx@msn.com. Once received, the researcher will send a confirmation e-mail back and remove participant from the study.
2. Your identity will be kept confidential.
3. The researcher, has fully explained the nature of the research study and has answered all of your questions and concerns.
4. If interviews are done, they may be recorded. If they are recorded, you must give permission for the researcher to record the interviews. You understand that the information from the recorded interviews may be transcribed. Data will be coded to assure that your identity is protected.
5. Data will be kept in a secure and locked area at (location noted) with single person access. After three years, the data collected and interview notes will be shredded, and tape recordings will be smashed and incinerated.
6. The results of this study may be published.

By signing this form, you agree that you understand the nature of the study, the possible risks to you as a participant, and how your identity will be kept confidential. When you sign this form, this means that you are 18 years old or older and that you give your permission to volunteer as a participant in the study that is described here.

( ) I accept the above terms.

( ) I do not accept the above terms. (check one)

Signature of the research participant
Date

Signature of the researcher
Date

Appendix C

Letter of Invitation

Dear (Name),

My name is Kenneth Jackson and because you are currently a doctoral mentor/professor at (Name of School), you have been chosen to be invited to participate in a research study entitled: Exploring Perceptions of Mentor Relationships in Doctoral Programs. The purpose of this research study is to explore doctoral candidates' mentor's perception on mentoring relationship experiences and student compatibility in doctoral programs.

The study will entail a tape-recorded, face-to-face interview that will last approximately one hour. I am requesting your participation in this study if you are a doctoral mentor / professor who has doctoral mentoring experience of three or more years. Your participation in this study will contribute knowledge to the study of mentoring relationships in doctoral programs.

You can be assured confidentiality. Your academic institution's information will be kept in the strictest confidence. Your participation is voluntary and you will need to read and agree to a consent form as a part of the interview. The interview will be held in a private location to ensure confidentiality of responses.

To participate, please sign to attest confirmation that you agree to adhere to maintaining the confidentiality and keeping your academic institutions information confidential and return it to me via email at xxxxxxx@msn.com.

If you have any questions, please contact me at (xxx)xxx-xxxx or by email at xxxxxxxxxxxxx@msn.com.

Thank you for your support.

Kenneth Jackson
Doctoral Student
University of Phoenix

_____
Signature

_____
Date

Appendix D

Interview Questions

1. How would you describe your role as a mentor in recent years?
2. How do you perceive your role as a doctoral mentor?
3. How important is the early phase of building a mentoring relationship with a mentee? Please elaborate and provide examples.
4. What type of indications and factors are associated with building an effective mentoring relationship during the initiation phase?
5. How important is cognitive development (i.e. writing, research skills, and developing new learning patterns) in mentees during the mentor/mentee relationship? Please elaborate.
6. How do you think a mentor's positive influence affects a mentee's cognitive development?
7. How do you think a mentor's lack of positive influence affect the cognitive development of mentees?
8. What are your feelings on the mentor/mentee matching process currently used at your university?
9. How does the university ensure compatibility when matching doctoral students with mentors?
10. What would help improve mentoring relationships?
11. Is there anything you can add to this discussion and study we have not touched on?

Appendix E

Field Test Letter of Invitation

Dear,

My name is Kenneth Jackson and because you are currently a doctoral mentor/professor at (Name of School), you have been chosen to be invited to participate in a field test of my interview questions for my research study entitled: Exploring Perceptions of Mentor Relationships in Doctoral Programs. The purpose of this research study is to explore doctoral mentors' perception on mentoring relationship experiences and student compatibility in doctoral programs.

Participation would involve providing feedback on the interview questions for clarity, comprehension, and readability and provide any feedback on improvement. The researcher will make revisions, adjustments, or refinements to the interview questions that are of concern from the field test. The field test will take approximately no more than 60 minutes to conduct.

You can be assured confidentiality. Your academic institution's information will be kept in the strictest confidence. Your participation is voluntary and you will need to read and agree to a consent form as a part of the field test.

To participate, please sign to attest confirmation that you agree to adhere to maintaining the confidentiality and keeping your academic institutions information confidential and return it to me via email at xxxxxx@msn.com. If you have any questions, please contact me at (xxx)xxx-xxxx or by email at xxxxxx@msn.com.

Thank you for your support.

Kenneth Jackson
Doctoral Student
University of Phoenix

_____
Signature

_____
Date

Appendix F

Revision of Interview Questions

Field Test Q1: How do you perceive your role as a mentor?
Final Revised Q1: How would you describe your role as a mentor in recent years?

Field Test Q2: How do you perceive your role as a doctoral mentor?
Final Revised Q2: No change.

Field Test Q3: How important is the initiation phase of building a mentoring relationship with a mentee?
Final Revised Q3: How important is the early phase of building a mentoring relationship with a mentee? Please elaborate and provide examples.

Field Test Q4: What type of indications is associated with being a good fit when building an effective mentoring relationship during the initiation phase?
Final Revised Q4: What type of indicators and factors are associated with building an effective mentoring relationship during the initiation phase?

Field Test Q5: How important is cognitive development in mentees during the mentor/mentee relationship?
Final Revised Q5: How important is cognitive development (i.e. writing, research skills, and developing new learning patterns) in mentees during the mentor/mentee relationship?

Field Test Q6: How do you think a mentor's influence enhances a mentee's cognitive development?

Final Revised Q6: How do you think a mentor's positive influence affect a mentee's cognitive development?

Field Test Q7: What are your feelings on the lack of a mentor's positive influence that may inhibit the cognitive development of mentees?
Final Revised Q7: How do you think a mentor's lack of positive influence affect the cognitive development of mentees?

Field Test Q8: What do you remember most about your experiences with the matching of a mentee?
Final Revised Q8: What are your feelings on the mentor / mentee matching process currently used at your university?

Field Test Q9: What are your feelings on the mentor/mentee?
Final Revised Q9: How does the university ensure compatibility when matching doctoral students with mentors?

Field Test Q10: How do you ensure compatibility when matching with a doctoral student?
Final Revised Q10: What would help improve mentoring relationships?

Field Test Q11: No initial question.
Final Revised Q11: Is there anything you can add to this discussion and study we have not touched on?

REFERENCES

Akanni, A. (2011). Mentoring relationship: A protégé experience. IFE Psychologia, 120-128. Retrieved from ajol.info/index.php/ifep

Alderfer, C. P. (2014). Clarifying the meaning of mentor–protégé relationships. Consulting Psychology Journal: Practice and Research, 66(1), 6-19. dx.doi.org/10.1037/a0036367

Allen, E. & Seaman, J. (2013). Changing course: Ten years of tracking online education in the United States. Babson Survey Research Group and Qualong Research Group. Retrieved from: babson.edu/Academics/faculty/provost/Pages/babson-survey- research-group.aspx

Al-Natour, A., Qandil, A., & Gillespie, G. L. (2015). Intimate partner violence screening barriers as perceived by Jordanian nurses: A qualitative descriptive study. Journal of Nursing Education and Practice, 5(9), 11-16. dx.doi.org/10.5430/jnep.v5n9p11

Ampaw, F. D., & Jaeger, A. J. (2012). Completing the three stages of doctoral education: An event history analysis. Research in Higher Education, 53(6), 640-660. dx.doi.org/10.1007/s11162-011-9250-3

Anastasia, T. T., PhD., Skinner, R. L., & Mundhenk, S. E., M.S. (2012). Youth mentoring: Program and mentor best practices. Journal of Family and Consumer Sciences, 104(2), 38-44. Retrieved from natefacs.org/JFCSE/jfcse.htm

Anderson, D., & Shore, W. (2008). Ethical issues and concerns associated with mentoring undergraduate students. Ethics & Behavior, 18(1), 1-25. doi:10.1080/10508420701519577

Anderson, S., & Anderson, B. (2012). Preparation and socialization of the education professoriate: Narratives of doctoral student-instructors. International Journal of Teaching and Learning in Higher Education, 24(2), 239-251. Retrieved from isetl.org/ijtlhe/

Anne Bogat, G., Liang, B., & Rigol-dahn, R. (2008). Stages of mentoring: An analysis of an intervention for pregnant and parenting adolescents. Child & Adolescent Social Work Journal, 25(4), 325-341. dx.doi.org/10.1007/s10560-008-0130-4

Aslan, B., & Öcal, S. D. (2012). A case study on mentoring in a teacher development program. Journal of Education and Future, 2, 31-48. Retrieved from http://oaji.net/journal-detail.html?number=320

Asokan, S., Surendran, S., Asokan, S., & Nuvvula, S. (2014). Relevance of Piaget's cognitive principles among 4-7 years old children: A descriptive cross-sectional study. Journal of the Indian Society of Pedodontics and Preventive Dentistry, 32(4), 292-6. dx.doi.org/10.4103/0970-4388.140947

Babbi, E. B. (2004). The practice of social research (10th ed.). Belmont, CA: Wadsworth/Thompson.

Ballamingie, P. & Mikeson, S., 2011, 'The vulnerable researcher: Some unanticipated challenges of doctoral fieldwork', The Qualitative Report, 16(3), 711-729. Retrieved from http://tqr.nova.edu/

Bandura, A. (1986). Social foundation of thought and action: A social-cognitive theory. Englewood Cliffs, NJ: Prentice-Hall.

Barnes, B. J., & Randall, J. (2012). Doctoral student satisfaction: An examination of disciplinary, enrollment, and institutional differences. Research in Higher Education, 53(1), 47-75. dx.doi.org/10.1007/s11162-011-9225-4

Barnetz, Z., & Feigin, R. (2012). "We didn't have to talk": Adolescent perception of mentor-mentee relationships in an evaluation study of a mentoring program for adolescents with juvenile diabetes. Child & Adolescent Social Work Journal, 29(6), 463-483. dx.doi.org/10.1007/s10560-012-0273-1

Barondess, J. A. (1995). President's address: A brief history of mentoring. American Clinical and Climatological Association, 106, 1-24. Retrieved from medicalarchives.jhmi.edu/climatologicalassociation.html

Barratt-Pugh, L. (2012). Mentoring the next researcher generation: Reflections on three years of building VET research capacity and infrastructure. International Journal of Training Research, 10(1), 6-22. Retrieved from tandfonline.com/loi/ritr

Baxter, P. & Jack, S. (2008). Qualitative case study methodology: Study design and implementation for novice researchers. The Qualitative Report, 13(4), 544-559. Retrieved from http://tqr.nova.edu/

Becher, T. (1989). Academic tribes and territories: Intellectual inquiry and the culture of the disciplines. Bristol, PA: Open University Press.

Belachew, D. (2012). How to get the most out of mentorship. Infectious Disease News, 25(2), 41. Retrieved from healio.com/infectious-disease

Bell, A., & Treleaven, L. (2011). Looking for professor right: Mentee selection of mentors in a formal mentoring program. Higher Education, 61(5), 545-561. dx.doi.org/10.1007/s10734-010-9348-0

Belle, R. R., Cotton, J. L., & Miller, J. S. (2000). Marginal mentoring: The effects of type of mentor, quality of relationship, and program desing on work and career attitudes. Academy of Management Journal, 43(6), 1177-1194. Retrieved from http://aom.org/amj/

Black, R. (2012). The dissertation marathon. Contemporary Issues in Education Research (Online), 5(2), 97-105. Retrieved from cluteinstitute.com/journals/contemporary-issues-in-education- research-cier/

Blickle, G.S., Schneider, P.B., Meurs, J.A. and Perrewé, P.L. (2010). Antecedents and consequences of perceived barriers to obtaining mentoring: a longitudinal investigation, Journal of Applied Social Psychology, 40(8), 1897-1920. Retrieved from http://onlinelibrary.wiley.com/journal/10.1111/%28ISSN%291559-1816

Bloomberg, L. D. & Volpe, M. F. (2008). Completing your qualitative dissertation: A roadmap from beginning to end. Los Angeles, CA: Sage.

Bolliger, D. U., & Halupa, C. (2012). Student perceptions of satisfaction and anxiety in an online doctoral program. Distance Education, 33(1), 81-98. Retrieved from tandfonline.com/toc/hajd20/current#.U3OYXGcQMVQ

Borst, G., Poirel, N., Pineau, A., Cassotti, M., & Houdé, O. (2013). Inhibitory control efficiency in a Piaget-like class-inclusion task in school-age children and adults: A developmental negative priming study. Developmental Psychology, 49(7), 1366-1374. dx.doi.org/10.1037/a0029622

Bozeman, B. & Feeney, M. K. (2008). Public management mentoring: What affects outcomes? Journal of Public Administration Research and Theory, 19, 427-452. Retrieved from https://jpart.oxfordjournals.org/

Brannagan, K. B., & Oriol, M. (2014). A model for orientation and mentoring of online adjunct faculty in nursing. Nursing Education Perspectives, 35(2), 128-130. doi.org/10.5480/1536-5026-35.2.128

Brill, S. & McCartney, A. (2008). Stopping the revolving door: Increasing teacher retention. Politics & Policy, 36(5), 750-774. Doi: https://doi.org/10.1111/j.1747- 1346.2008.00133.x

Brill, J. L., Balcanoff, K. K., Land, D., Gogarty, M. M., & Turner, F. (2014). Best practices in doctoral retention: Mentoring. Higher Learning Research Communications, 4(2), 26-37. Retrieved from hlrcjournal.com/index.php/HLRC

Brondyk, S., & Searby, L. (2013). Best practices in mentoring: Complexities and possibilities. International Journal of Mentoring and Coaching in Education, 2(3), 189-203. Retrieved from emccouncil.org/eu/en/journal

Brooks, C. (2012, December 03). How to be a good mentor. Business News Daily. Retrieved from businessnewsdaily.com/3504-how-to-mentor.html

Broughton, W. (1991). Qualitative methods in program evaluation. American Journal of Health Promotion, 6(6), 461-465. Retrieved from www.healthpromotionjournal.com/

Bryant-Shanklin, M. & Brumage, N. W. (2011). Collaborative responsive education mentoring: Mentoring for professional development in higher education. Florida Journal of Educational Administration & Policy, 5(1), 42-53. Retrieved from http://education.ufl.edu/fjeap/

Burmester, L. M., Metscher, D. S., & Smith, M. L. (2014). Analysis of contributing factors to high attrition rates in online educational programs. International Journal of Professional Aviation Training & Testing Research, 6(1), 1-17. Retrieved from http://ojs.library.okstate.edu/osu/index.php/IJPATTR

Butler, A. J., Whiteman, R. S., & Crow, G. M. (2013). Technology's role in fostering transformational educator mentoring. International Journal of Mentoring and Coaching in Education, 2(3), 233-248. Retrieved from emccouncil.org/eu/en/journal

Buzatu, N., & Pipas, M. (2014). Effective communication - A viable solution to mediation. International Journal of Academic Research in Business and Social Sciences, 4(1), 681-685. Retrieved from http://hrmars.com/index.php/pages/detail/IJARBSS

Callary, B., Werthner, P., & Trudel, P. (2012). The lived experience of a doctoral student: The process of learning and becoming. The Qualitative Report, 17(43), 1-20. Retrieved from http://tqr.nova.edu/

Campbell, C. M., Smith, M., Dugan, J. P., & Komives, S. R. (2012). Mentors and college student leadership outcomes: The importance of position and process. Review of Higher Education, 35(4), 595-625. doi: https://doi.org/10.1353/rhe.2012.0037

Cao, G. (2007). The pattern-matching role of systems thinking in improving research trustworthiness. Systemic Practice and Action Research, 20(6), 441-453. dx.doi.org/10.1007/s11213-007-9069-1

Cassuto, L. (2013, July 01). PhD attrition: How much is too much? A disturbing 50 percent of doctoral students leave graduate school without finishing. Retrieved from chronicle.com/?cid=UCHETOPNAV

Chao, G. T. (1997). Mentoring phases and outcomes. Journal of Vocational Behavior, 51, 15–28. doi: https://doi.org/10.1006/jvbe.1997.1591

Christensen, L. B., Johnson, R. B., & Turner, L. A. (2011). Research methods, design, and analysis (11th ed.). Boston, MA: Allyn & Bacon.

Chun, J., Sosik, J. J., & Yun, N. (2012). A longitudinal study of mentor and protégé outcomes in formal mentoring relationships. Journal of Organizational Behavior, 33(8), 1071-1094. doi:10.1002/job.1781

Columbaro, N. L. (2015). Paving the way toward faculty careers in higher education: Student mentoring relationship experiences while completing online doctoral degrees. Retrieved from newprairiepress.org/aerc/?utm_source=newprairiepress.org%2Faerc%2F2016%2Froundtables%2F3&utm_medium=PDF&utm_campaign=PDFCoverPages

Cornelius, V. E., & Wood, L. N. (2012). Academic to student mentoring within a large Australian business school. Asian Social Science, 8(14), 1-8. Retrieved from doi: https://doi.org/10.5539/ass.v8n14p1

Cowin, K.M., Cohen, L.M., Ciechanowski, K.M. and Orozco, R.A. (2012). Portraits of mentor-junior faculty relationships: from power dynamics to collaboration. Journal of Education, 192(1), 37-47. Retrieved from bu.edu/journalofeducation/

Culp, B. & Urtel, M. (2013). Demonstrating successful undergraduate research experiences across the disciplines: The physical education teacher education perspective. Journal of Physical Education, Recreation & Dance, 84(9), 24-27. Retrieved from doi.org/10.1080/07303084.2013.838111

Cynthia, G. C., Renold, L. C., Ahmed, S., Lee, J., Carter-Wells, J., Worden, M., . . . Schools, J. (2012). Video conferencing guidelines for faculty and students in graduate online courses. Journal of Online Learning and Teaching, 8(4), 277-287. Retrieved from http://jolt.merlot.org/

Davis, D. (2007). Access to academe: The importance of mentoring to black students. Negro Educational Review, 58(3/4), 217-231. Retrieved from http://thener.org/

Delaney, Y. A. (2012). Research on mentoring language teachers: Its role in language education. Foreign Language Annals, 45(1), S184-S202. Retrieved from doi: https://doi.org/10.1111/j.1944-9720.2011.01185.x

Delmar, C. (2010). Generalizability as recognition: Reflection on a foundational problem in qualitative research. Qualitative Studies, 1(2), 115-128. Retrieved from http://ojs.statsbiblioteket.dk/index.php/qual/index

DeMoss, W. L., Clem, B. C., & Wilson, K. (2012). Using technology to mentor aspiring LSLS professionals. The Volta Review, 112(3), 329-343. Retrieved from https://www.agbell.org/TheVoltaReview/

Denzin, N. K., & Lincoln, Y. S. (Eds.). (1994). Handbook of qualitative research. Thousand Oaks, CA: Sage.

Di Pierro, M. (2012). Strategies for doctoral student retention: Taking the roads less traveled. The Journal for Quality and Participation, 35(3), 29-32. Retrieved from http://asq.org/pub/jqp/

Doloriert, C., Sambrook, S., & Stewart, J. (2012). Power and emotion in doctoral supervision: Implications for HRD. European Journal of Training and Development, 36(7), 732-750. dx.doi.org/10.1108/03090591211255566

Dominguez, N., & Hager, M. (2013). Mentoring frameworks: Synthesis and critique. International Journal of Mentoring and Coaching in Education, 2(3), 171-188. Retrieved from doi: https://doi.org/10.1108/IJMCE-03-2013-0014

Dow, R. S. (2014). Leadership responsibility in mentoring organization newcomers. Journal of Management Policy and Practice, 15(1), 104-112. Retrieved from http://jmppnet.com/

Drost, E. (2011). Validity and reliability in social science research. Education Research & Perspectives, 38(1), 105-123. Retrieved from erpjournal.net/

Dreyer, C. L. (2014). Group cooperation and the mentor-mentee relationship in undergraduate research. Research Quarterly for Exercise and Sport, 85, 1. Retrieved from tandfonline.com/toc/urqe20/current

Dunnagan, T., Peterson, M., & Wilson, J. (1997). Qualitative evaluation techniques and wellness programming. American Journal of Health Studies, 13(4), 205-214. Retrieved from va-ajhs.com/

Durlak, J. A., Weissberg, R. P., Dymnicki, A. B., Taylor, R. D., & Schellinger, K. B. (2011). The impact of enhancing students' social and emotional learning: A meta-analysis of school-based universal interventions. Child Development, 82(1), 405-432. Retrieved from doi: https://doi.org/10.1111/j.1467-8624.2010.01564.x

Eby, L., Butts, M., Lockwood, A., & Simon, S. A. (2004). Protégés' negative mentoring experiences: Construct development and nomological validation. Personnel Psychology, 57(2), 411-447. Retrieved from doi: https://doi.org/10.1111/j.1744- 6570.2004.tb02496.x

Eby, L. T. d. T., Allen, T. D., Hoffman, B. J., Baranik, L. E., Sauer, J. B., Baldwin, S., Evans, S. C. (2013). An interdisciplinary meta-analysis of the potential antecedents, correlates, and consequences of protégé perceptions of mentoring. Psychological Bulletin, 139(2), 441-476. dx.doi.org/10.1037/a0029279

Elizabeth, T. W., Bhave, D., & Kyoung, y. K. (2012). Are you my mentor? Informal mentoring mutual identification. Career Development International, 17(2), 137- 148. dx.doi.org/10.1108/13620431211225322

Encyclopedia of Children's Health (2015). Cognitive development. Retrieved from healthofchildren.com/C/Cognitive-Development.html

Erikson, E. (1950). Childhood and Society. New York: Norton

Erlen, J. A. (2010). Informed consent: Revisiting the issues. Orthopaedic Nursing, 29(4), 276-80. Retrieved from doi: https://doi.org/10.1097/NOR.0b013e3181e517f1

Evans, D. (2007). Learning to be a leader/mentor. Mentoring & Tutoring: Partnership in Learning, 15(4), 385-390. doi: https://doi.org/10.1080/13611260701658944

Evans, R. R., & Forbes, L. (2012). Mentoring the 'net generation': Faculty perspectives in health education. College Student Journal, 46(2), 397-404. Retrieved from projectinnovation.com/home.html

Ewing, J. C., Foster, D. D., & Whittington, M. S. (2011). Explaining student cognition during class sessions in the context Piaget's theory of cognitive development. NACTA Journal, 55(1), 68-75. Retrived from https://www.nactateachers.org/

Ewing, H., Mathieson, K., Alexander, J. L., & Leafman, J. (2012). Enhancing the acquisition of research skills in online doctoral programs: The Ewing model. Journal of Online Learning and Teaching, 8(1), 34. Retrieved from http://jolt.merlot.org/

Ezebilo, E. E. (2012). Challenges in postgraduate studies: Assessments by doctoral students in a Swedish university. Higher Education Studies, 2(4), 49-57. Retrieved from doi.org/10.5539/hes.v2n4p49

Fedler, F. (1996). Mentoring manual for teaching the culture of the field. Journalism & Mass Communication Educator, 51(3), 74-80. Retrieved from

doi.org/10.1177/107769589605100309
Firestone, W. A. (1987). Meaning in method: The rhetoric of quantitative and qualitative research. Educational Researcher, 16 (7), 16 – 21. Retrieved from doi.org/10.3102/0013189X016007016
Fischer, C. (2013). Trust and communication in European agri-food chains. Supply Chain Management, 18(2), 208-218. dx.doi.org/10.1108/13598541311318836
Fletcher, S. & Mullen, C. (2012). Sage handbook of mentoring and coaching in education. Thousand Oaks, CA: Sage.
Forehand, R. (2008). The art and science of mentoring in psychology: A necessary practice to ensure our future. American Psychologist, 63(8), 744-755. Retrieved from doi.org/10.1037/0003-066X.63.8.744
Fowler, R. M. (2013). "When you want to give up, you want to give in": Mentoring perceptions of African American women doctoral students at a predominately white institution. Retrieved from ProQuest Dissertations and Theses. UMI No. 3607432
Fragoulis, I., Dr, Valkanos, E., Dr, & Voula, F. (2011). Research of executives' perceptions in companies and organizations on the importance of mentoring in the frame of in-house education and training. International Education Studies, 4(3), 109-118. Retrieved from doi.org/10.5539/ies.v4n3p109
Francois, E. J., PhD. (2014). Motivational orientations of non-traditional adult students to enroll in a degree-seeking program. New Horizons in Adult Education & Human Resource Development, 26(2), 19-35. Retrieved from doi.org/10.1002/nha3.20060
Froehlich, H. (2012). Mentoring doctoral students in music education: Personal reflections about ethical choices and conflicts in higher education. Action, Criticism & Theory for Music Education, 11(1), 43-61. Retrieved from http://act.maydaygroup.org/
Gaiter, D. J. (2013). Facets of leadership. The Neurodiagnostic Journal, 53(4), 323-7. Retrieved from aset.org/i4a/pages/index.cfm?pageid=3314
Gardner, S. (2008). "What's too much and what's too little? The process of becoming an independent researcher in doctoral education. Journal of Higher Education, 79(3), 326–350. Retrieved from https://ohiostatepress.org/JHE.html
Gardner, S. K. (2010). Fitting the mold of graduate school: A qualitative study of socialization in doctoral education. Innovations in Higher Education, 33, 125– 138. http://dx.doi.org/10.1007/s10755-008-9068-x
Gasson, S., & Waters, J. (2013). Using a grounded theory approach to study online collaboration behaviors. European Journal of Information Systems, 22(1), 95-118. dx.doi.org/10.1057/ejis.2011.24
Gay, B. (1994). What is mentoring? Education & Training, 36(5), 4-7. Retrieved from doi.org/10.1108/00400919410062257
George, M. P., & Sebastian, R. M. (2012). A model for student mentoring in business schools. International Journal of Mentoring and Coaching in Education, 1(2), 136-154. dx.doi.org/10.1108/20466851211262879
Gilles, C., Carrillo, L. T., Wang, Y., Stegall, J., & Bumgarner, B. (2013). "Working with my mentor is like having a second brain/hands/feet/eyes": Perceptions of novice teachers. English Journal, 102(3), 78-86. Retrieved from www.ncte.org/journals/ej
Glanville, C., & Porche, D. (2000). Graduate nursing faculty: Ensuring cultural and racial diversity through faculty development. Journal of Multicultural Nursing & Health, 6(1), 6-13. Retrieved from https://catalyst.library.jhu.edu/catalog/bib_3561686
Glaser, J. & Laudel, G. (2013). Life with and without coding: Two methods for early- stage data analysis in qualitative research aiming at casual explanations. Qualitative Social Research, 14(2), 1-37. Retrieved from qualitative-research.net/index.php/fqs/issue/archive
Goodyear, M. (2009). Mentoring: A learning collaboration. Educause Quarterly Magazine, 29(4), 51-53. Retrieved from educause.edu/
Gordon, J., Downey, J., & Bangert, A. (2013). Effects of a school-based mentoring program on school behavior and measures of adolescent connectedness. School Community Journal, 23(2), 227-249. Retrieved from schoolcommunitynetwork.org/SCJ.aspx
Gray, D. (2013). Barriers to online postsecondary education crumble: Enrollment in traditional face-to-face courses declines as enrollment in online courses increases. Contemporary

Issues in Education Research (Online), 6(3), 345-349. Retrieved from doi.org/10.19030/cier.v6i3.8537

Guise, M., & Fink, L. S., R.W.T. (2013). Forming university and teacher partnerships in an effort to reframe and rethink mentoring programs. English Journal, 102(3), 65-70. Retrieved from ncte.org/journals/ej

Gutiérrez, L. M. (2012). Recognizing and valuing our roles as mentors. Journal of Social Work Education, 48(1), 1-4. Retrieved from doi.org/10.5175/JSWE.2012.334800001

Hagemeier, N. E, Murawski, M. M., & Popovich, N. G. (2013). The influence of faculty mentors on junior pharmacy faculty members' career decisions. American Journal of Pharmaceutical Education, 77(3), 1-51. Retrieved from doi.org/10.5688/ajpe77351

Hafen, C. A., Allen, J. P., Mikami, A. Y., Gregory, A., Hamre, B., & Pianta, R. C. (2012). The pivotal role of adolescent autonomy in secondary school classrooms. Journal of Youth and Adolescence, 41(3), 245-255. dx.doi.org/10.1007/s10964-011-9739-2

Haggard, D. L. (2012). Mentoring and psychological contract breach. Journal of Business and Psychology, 27(2), 161-175. dx.doi.org/10.1007/s10869-011-9237-2

Hall, E. L. & Maltby, L. E. (2013). Mentoring: The view from both sides. Journal of Psychology and Christianity, 32(1), 70-74. Retrieved from doi.org/10.1201/b15518-18

Hallam, P. R., (Felipe) Chou, P. N., Hite, J. M., & Hite, S. J. (2012). Two contrasting models for mentoring as they affect retention of beginning teachers. National Association of Secondary School Principals.NASSP Bulletin, 96(3), 243-278. Retrieved from doi.org/10.1177/0192636512447132

Hamlin, R. G., & Sage, L. (2011). Behavioural criteria of perceived mentoring effectiveness. Journal of European Industrial Training, 35(8), 752-778. dx.doi.org/10.1108/03090591111168311

Harris, C. S. (2011). The case for partnering doctoral students with librarians: A synthesis of the literatures. Library Review, 60(7), 599-620. dx.doi.org/10.1108/00242531111153614

Healy, N. A., Cantillon, P., Malone, C., & Kerin, M. J. (2012). Role models and mentors in surgery. The American Journal of Surgery, 204(2), 256-61. dx.doi.org/10.1016/j.amjsurg.2011.09.031

Hegarty, N., & Del Vecchio, R. (2012). The disconnect between workplace and graduate school motivation - exploring the life motivation continuum. The Business Review, Cambridge, 19(2), 26-33. Retrieved from jaabc.com/brc.html

Hellsten, L. M., Prytula, M. P., Ebanks, A., & Lai, H. (2009). Teacher induction: Exploring beginning teacher mentorship. Canadian Journal of Education, 32(4), 703-733. Retrieved from csse-scee.ca/CJE/

Hezlett, S. A. (2005). Protégés' learning in mentoring relationships: A review of the literature and an exploratory case study. Advances in Developing Human Resources, 7(4), 505-526. Retrieved from doi.org/10.1177/1523422305279686

Hills, L., D.A. (2013). What to do when trust has been breached in your practice. The Journal of Medical Practice Management: MPM, 29(3), 199-203. Retrieved from https://www.greenbranch.com/store/index.cfm/product/4_15/the-journal-of- medical-practice-managementsupregsup.cfm

Holley, K. A., & Caldwell, M. L. (2012). The challenges of designing and implementing a doctoral student mentoring program. Innovative Higher Education, 37(3), 243- 253. dx.doi.org/10.1007/s10755-011-9203-y

Holloway, L, & Wheeler, S. (2002). Qualitative research in nursing. Malden, MA: Blackwell.

Horowitz, J., & Christopher, K. B. (2013). The research mentoring program: Serving the needs of graduate and undergraduate researchers. Innovative Higher Education, 38(2), 105-116. dx.doi.org/10.1007/s10755-012-9230-3

Houser, C., Lemmons, K., & Cahill, A. (2013). Role of the faculty mentor in an undergraduate research experience. Journal of Geoscience Education, 61(3), 297-305. Retrieved from journalofgeoscienceeducation.org/ Hovdhaugen, E. (2011). Do structured study programmes lead to lower rates of dropout and student transfer from university? Irish Educational Studies, 30(2), 237-251. Retrieved from doi.org/10.1080/03323315.2011.569143

Howard, A., & Hirani, K. (2013). Transformational change and stages of development in the workplace. Journal of Integral Theory and Practice, 8(1), 71-86. Retrieved from https://foundation.metaintegral.org/jitp

Howcroft, D., & McDonald, R. (2007). An ethnographic study of IS investment appraisal. International Journal of Technology and Human Interaction, 3(3), 69-86. Retrieved from doi.org/10.4018/jthi.2007070106

Hrastinski, S., & Jaldemark, J. (2012). How and why do students of higher education participate in online seminars? Education and Information Technologies, 17(3), 253-271. dx.doi.org/10.1007/s10639-011-9155-y

Hu, C., Thomas, K. & Lance, C. (2008). Intentions to initiate mentoring relationships: Understanding the impact of race, proactivity, feelings of deprivation, and relationship roles. Journal of Social Psychology, 148(6), 727-744. Retrieved from doi.org/10.3200/SOCP.148.6.727-744

Huang, C., & Weng, R. (2012). Exploring the antecedents and consequences of mentoring relationship effectiveness in the healthcare environment. Journal of Management and Organization, 18(5), 685-701. Retrieved from doi.org/10.5172/jmo.2012.18.5.685

Hurd, N. M., Varner, F. A., & Rowley, S. J. (2013). Involved-vigilant parenting and socio-emotional well-being among black youth: The moderating influence of natural mentoring relationships. Journal of Youth and Adolescence, 42(10), 1583- 95. dx.doi.org/10.1007/s10964-012-9819-y

Huskins, W., Silet, K., Weber-Main, A., Begg, M. D., Fowler, J. G., Hamilton, J., & Fleming, M. (2011). Identifying and Aligning Expectations in a Mentoring Relationship. CTS: Clinical & Translational Science, 4(6), 439-447. doi:10.1111/j.1752-8062.2011.00356.x

Iacovelli, A. M., & Johnson, C. (2012). Disclosure through face-to-face and instant messaging modalities: Psychological and physiological effects. Journal of Social and Clinical Psychology, 31(3), 225-250. dx.doi.org/101521jscp2012313225

Ifenthaler, D., Masduki, I., & Seel, N. M. (2011). The mystery of cognitive structure and how we can detect it: Tracking the development of cognitive structures over time. Instructional Science, 39(1), 41-61. dx.doi.org/10.1007/s11251-009-9097-6

Johnson, W. B. (2002). The intentional mentor: Strategies and guidelines for the practice of mentoring. Professional Psychology: Research and Practice, 33(1), 88-96. dx.doi.org/10.1037/0735-7028.33.1.88

Joo, B., Sushko, J. S., & McLean, G. N. (2012). Multiple faces of coaching: Manager-as-coach, executive coaching, and formal mentoring. Organization Development Journal, 30(1), 19-38. Retrieved from isodc.org/page-1730212

Jordan, J. V. (2013). The power of connection: Recent developments in relational- cultural theory. New York, NY: Routledge.

Jor'dan, J. R., Muñoz, M., Figlar, M., & Rust, F. O. (2013). Creating space: Leader development in early childhood education. YC Young Children, 68(1), 62-66. Retrieved from naeyc.org/yc/

Joshith, V. P. (2012). Emotional intelligence as a tool for innovative teaching. I- Manager's Journal on Educational Psychology, 5(4), 54-60. Retrieved from imanagerpublications.com/

Kahle-Piasecki, L. (2011). Making a mentoring relationship work: What is required for organizational success. The Journal of Applied Business and Economics, 12(1), 46-56. Retrieved from aebrjournal.org/

Karcher, M. J., Nakkula, M. J., & Harris, J. (2005). Developmental mentoring match characteristics: Correspondence between mentors' and mentees' assessments of relationship quality. Journal of Primary Prevention, 26(2), 93-110. dx.doi.org/10.1007/s10935-005-1847-x

Kayama, M., Gregg, M. F., Asahara, K., Yamamoto-Mitani, N., Okuma, K., Ohta, K., & Kinoshita, Y. (2013). Mentoring doctoral students for qualitative research: Interviews with experienced nursing faculty in japan. Journal of Nursing Education, 52(5), 283-289. dx.doi.org/10.3928/01484834-20130320-02

Keller, T. E., & Pryce, J. M. (2012). Different roles and different results: How activity orientations correspond to relationship quality and student outcomes in school- based mentoring. Journal of Primary Prevention, 33(1), 47-64. dx.doi.org/10.1007/s10935-012-0264-1

Kennedy, D. H., Terrell, S. R., & Lohle, M. (2015). A grounded theory of persistence in a limited-residency doctoral program. The Qualitative Report, 20(3), 215-230. Retrieved from http://tqr.nova.edu/

Kent, A. M., Kochan, F., & Green, A. M. (2013). Cultural influences on mentoring programs and relationships: A critical review of research. International Journal of Mentoring and Coaching in Education, 2(3), 204-217. Retrieved from doi.org/10.1108/IJMCE-08-2013-0047

Kern, M. K. (2013). I'm a chair, but I feel like a folding chair. Reference & User Services Quarterly, 53(1), 5-8. Retrieved from doi.org/10.5860/rusq.53n1.5

Khosla, R. (2013). A case study of mentoring at ONGC. Review of HRM, 2, 290-298. Retrieved from jhrm.eu/

Kiersma, M. E, Hagemeier, N., Chen, A. H., Melton, B., Noureldin, M., M. S., & Plake, K. S. (2012). A graduate student mentoring program to develop interest in research. American Journal of Pharmaceutical Education, 76(6), 1-104. Retrieved from http://archive.ajpe.org/about.asp

Kiran, V., Majumdar, M., & Kishore, K. (2012). Mentoring: A differentiating factor in management education business. Asia Pacific Journal of Management & Entrepreneurship Research, 1(2), 25-41. Retrieved from apjmer.org/

Knouse, S. B. (2013). Mentoring for Hispanics. Review of Business, 33(2), 80-90. Retrieved from stjohns.edu/

Kogan, S. M., Brody, G. H., & Chen, Y.-f. (2011). Natural mentoring processes deter externalizing problems among rural African American emerging adults: A prospective analysis. American Journal of Community Psychology, 48(3-4), 272-283. Retrieved from doi.org/10.1007/s10464-011-9425-2

Koocher, G. P. (2002). Mentor revealed: Masculinization of an early feminist construct. Professional Psychology: Research and Practice, 33(5), 509-510. Retrieved from doi.org/10.1037/0735-7028.33.5.509

Kram, K.E. (1983). Phases of the mentor relationship. Academy of Management Journal, 26(4), 608-625. Retrieved from http://amj.aom.org/

Kram, K. E. (1985). Mentoring at work: Developmental relationships in organizational life. Glenview, IL: Scott, Foresman.

Krause-Parello, C., Sarcone, A., Samms, K., & Boyd, Z. N. (2013). Developing a center for nursing research: An influence on nursing education and research through mentorship. Nurse Education in Practice, 13(2), 106-112. dx.doi.org/10.1016/j.nepr.2012.08.004

Laiho, M., & Brandt, T. (2012). Views of HR specialists on formal mentoring: Current situation and prospects for the future. Career Development International, 17(5), 435-457. dx.doi.org/10.1108/13620431211269694

Laughlin, K., & Moore, H. (2012). Mentoring and leadership: A practical application for one's career path. Journal of Adult Education, 41(1), 34-40. Retrieved from https://www.questia.com/library/p436763/journal-of-adult-education

Lechuga, V. M. (2011). Faculty-graduate student mentoring relationships: Mentors' perceived roles and responsibilities. Higher Education, 62(6), 757-771. dx.doi.org/10.1007/s10734-011-9416-0

Leck, J. D., Elliott, C., & Rockwell, B. (2012). E-mentoring women: Lessons learned from a pilot program. Journal of Diversity Management (Online), 7(2), 83. Retrieved from doi.org/10.19030/jdm.v7i2.7476

Leedy, P. D. & Ormrod, J. E. (2010). Practical research: Planning and design (9th ed.). Upper Saddle River, NJ: Prentice Hall.

Leshem, S. (2012). The many faces of mentor-mentee relationships in a pre-service teacher education programme. Creative Education, 3(4), 413-421. Retrieved from doi.org/10.4236/ce.2012.34065

Levinson, D. J., Darrow, C. N., Klein, E. B. Levinson, M. A. & McKee, B. (1978). Seasons of a man's life. New York, NY: Knopf.

Ligadu, C. P. (2012). The impact of the professional learning and psychological mentoring support for teacher trainees. Journal of Social Sciences, 8(3), 350-363. Retrieved from doi.org/10.3844/jssp.2012.350.363

Lightsey, R. (1999). Albert Bandura and the exercise of self-efficacy. Journal of Cognitive Psychotherapy, 13(2), 158-166. Retrieved from https://www.questia.com/library/p61764/journal-of-cognitive-psychotherapy

Lincoln, Y. S. & Guba, E. G. (1985). Naturalistic inquiry. Newbury Park, CA: Sage.

Liu, S., Yin, M., & Huang, T. (2013). Adolescents' interpersonal relationships with friends, parents, and teachers when using Facebook for interaction. Creative Education, 4(5), 335-339. Retrieved from doi.org/10.4236/ce.2013.45049

Lloyd, S. A., Byrne, M. M., & McCoy, T. S. (2012). Faculty-perceived barriers of online education. Journal of Online Learning and Teaching, 8(1), 1. Retrieved from http://jolt.merlot.org/

Lofthouse, R., & Wright, D. (2012). Teacher education lesson observation as boundary crossing. International Journal of Mentoring and Coaching in Education, 1(2), 89-103. dx.doi.org/10.1108/20466851211262842

Lorentzon, M. & Brown, K. (2003). Florence Nightingale as "mentor of matrons": Correspondence with Rachel Williams at St. Mary's Hospital. Journal of Nursing Management, 11(4), 266-274. doi: 10.1046/j.1365-2834.2003.00375.x

Lundgren, J. D., PhD., & Orsillo, S. M., PhD. (2012). The science and practice of mentoring in psychology doctoral training. Journal of Cognitive Psychotherapy, 26(3), 196-209. Retrieved from doi.org/10.1891/0889-8391.26.3.196

Lunsford, L. G. (2011). Psychology of mentoring: The case of talented college students. Journal of Advanced Academics, 22(3), 474-498,546-547. Retrieved from doi.org/10.1177/1932202x1102200305

Lunsford, L. G. (2014). Mentors, tormentors, and no mentors: Mentoring scientists. International Journal of Mentoring and Coaching in Education, 3(1), 4-17. Retrieved from doi.org/10.1108/IJMCE-02-2013-0007

Madhan, B., Ojha, A., & Gayathri, H. (2011). Perceived sources of psychological stress in post-graduate orthodontic students in India: A multicenter survey. Journal of International Dental and Medical Research, 4(3), 123-131. Retrieved from issuu.com/jidmr/docs/jidmr

Maher, M., & Macallister, H. (2013). Retention and attrition of students in higher education: Challenges in modern times to what works. Higher Education Studies, 3(2), 62-73. Retrieved from doi.org/10.5539/hes.v3n2p62

Makewa, L., Role, E., & Tuguta, E. (2013). Students' perceived level of English proficiency in secondary schools in Dodoma, Tanzania. International Journal of Instruction, 6(2), 35-52. Retrieved from http://e-iji.net/

Maldonado, V., Wiggers, R., & Arnold, C. (2013). So you want to earn a Phd? The attraction, realities, and outcomes of pursuing a doctorate. Toronto, ON: Higher Education Quality Council of Ontario.

Malmgren, R. D., Ottino, J. M., & Amaral, L. A. N. (2010). The role of mentorship in protégé performance. Nature, 465(7298), 622-627. Retrieved from doi.org/10.1038/nature09040

Marriott, S. (2006). A guide to coaching and mentoring. Nursing Management, 12(10), 1-18. Retrieved from http://journals.lww.com/nursingmanagement/pages/default.aspx

Martin, A. (2002). Transformational learning through mentoring in early childhood education: The DART model. In F. K. Kochan (Ed.), the organizational and human dimension of successful mentoring across diverse settings. Greenwich, CT: Information Age.

Martin, A. (2013). Downturn still squeezes colleges and universities. New York Times. Retrieved from: nytimes.com/2013/01/11/business/colleges-expect-lower-enrollment.html

Mavrinac, M. A. (2005). Transformational leadership: Peer mentoring as a values-based learning process. Portal: Libraries and the Academy, 5(3), 391-404. Retrieved from doi.org/10.1353/pla.2005.0037

May-Chiun Lo, & Ramayah, T. (2011). Mentoring and job satisfaction in Malaysian SMEs. The Journal of Management Development, 30(4), 427-440. dx.doi.org/10.1108/02621711111126891

McCallum, H. (2013). Students in the perioperative learning environment and emotional support. The Journal of Perioperative Practice, 23(7), 158-62. Retrieved from https://www.afpp.org.uk/home

McDowell, A. M., & Higbee, J. L. (2014). Responding to the concerns of student cultural groups: Redesigning spaces for cultural centers. Contemporary Issues in Education

Research (Online), 7(3), 227-236. Retrieved from doi.org/10.19030/cier.v7i3.8643

McKeage, R., Tischler, L., & Biberman, J. (2013). Improving student mentoring through meditation. Journal of American Academy of Business, Cambridge, 18(2), 210-217. Retrieved from jaabc.com/

McLeod, S. (2015). Jean Piaget. Retrieved from simplypsychology.org/ Mentee (2014). In Merriam-Webster Online. Retrieved from merriam-webster.com/dictionary/mentee

Merriam, S. B. (2009). Qualitative Research: A guide to design and implementation (2nd ed.). San Francisco, CA: Jossey-Bass.

Merriweather, L. R., & Morgan, A. J. (2013). Two cultures collide: Bridging the generation gap in a non-traditional mentorship. The Qualitative Report, 18(6), 1-16. Retrieved from http://tqr.nova.edu/

Metzger, A. H., Hardy, Y. M., Jarvis, C., Stoner, S. C., Pitlick, M., Hilaire, M. L., Hanes, S., Burke, J., & Lodise, N. M. (2013). Essential elements for a pharmacy practice mentoring program. American Journal of Pharmaceutical Education, 77(2), 3-23. Retrieved from doi.org/10.5688/ajpe77223

Meyer, M., & Warren-Gordon, K. (2013). Marginal mentoring in the contact space: Diversified mentoring relationships at a midsized Midwestern state university (MMSU). The Qualitative Report, 18(19), 1-18. Retrieved from Retrieved from http://tqr.nova.edu/

Michael, K. (2012). Virtual classroom: Reflections of online learning. Campus - Wide Information Systems, 29(3), 156-165. dx.doi.org/10.1108/10650741211243175

Miller, F. G. (2014). Clinical research before informed consent. Kennedy Institute of Ethics Journal, 24(2), 141-57. Retrieved from doi.org/10.1353/ken.2014.0009

Morse, J. M. (1995). The significance of saturation. Qualitative Health Research, 5(2), 147-149. Retrieved from doi.org/10.1177/104973239500500201

Morton, S. (2013). What support do health visitor mentors need? Community Practitioner, 86(8), 32-35. Retrieved from communitypractitioner.com/

Mullen, C. A. (2007). Trainers, illusionists, tricksters, and escapists: Changing the doctoral circus. The Educational Forum, 71(4), 300-315. Retrieved from doi.org/10.1080/00131720709335021

Mundia, C. N., & Iravo, M., Dr. (2014). Role of mentoring programs on the employee performance in organisations: A survey of public universities in Nyeri County, Kenya. International Journal of Academic Research in Business and Social Sciences, 4(8), 393-412. Retrieved from doi.org/10.6007/IJARBSS/v4- i8/1110

Munn, Z., Porritt, K., Lockwood, C., Aromataris, E., & Pearson, A. (2014). Establishing confidence in the output of qualitative research synthesis: The ConQual approach. BMC Medical Research Methodology, 14 dx.doi.org/10.1186/1471- 2288-14-108

Myers, J. B. (2012). Reflections of an ECT intern: Mentoring, leadership, and support. TechTrends, 56(2), 7-8. doi:http://dx.doi.org/10.1007/s11528-012-0556-6 Nadelson, S. G., & Nadelson, L. S. (2012). In search of the right book: Considerations in common read book selection. Journal of College Reading and Learning, 43(1), 60-66. Retrieved from doi.org/10.1080/10790195.2012.10850362

Nakanjako, D., Katamba, A., Kaye, D. K., Okello, E., Kamya, M. R., Sewankambo, N., & Mayanja-Kizza, H. (2014). Doctoral training in Uganda: Evaluation of mentoring best practices at makerere university college of health sciences. BMC Medical Education, 14, 9. dx.doi.org/10.1186/1472-6920-14-9

Neuman, W. L. (2011). Social research methods: Qualitative and quantitative approaches (7th ed.). Boston, MA: Pearson/Allyn & Bacon.

Noe, R. A. (1988). An investigation of the determinants of successful assigned mentoring relationships. Personnel Psychology, 41, 457–479. Retrieved from doi.org/10.1111/j.1744-6570.1988.tb00638.x

NVivo (2013). NVivo. Retrieved from www.qsrinternational.com/products_NVivo.aspx

O'Dell, S. J. (1990). Mentor teachers program. Washington, D.C.: National Educational Association.

O'Keeffe, P. (2013). A sense of belonging: Improving student retention. College Student Journal, 47(4), 605-613. Retrieved from projectinnovation.com/

Olivares, O. J. (2008). The formulation of a leadership development praxis: Linking intentions to outcomes. Leadership & Organization Development Journal, 29(6), 530-543.

dx.doi.org/10.1108/01437730810894186
O'Meara, K., Knudsen, K., & Jones, J. (2013). The role of emotional competencies in faculty-doctoral student relationships. Review of Higher Education, 36(3), 315-347. Retrieved from doi.org/10.1353/rhe.2013.0021

Opayemi, R. (2012). Psychosocial factors predisposing university undergraduates to mentoring relationship. Ife Psychologia, 20(1), 70-86. Retrieved from http://ifepsychologia.org/

Ortiz-Walters, R., & Gilson, L. L. (2005). Mentoring in academia: An examination of the experiences of protégés of color. Journal of Vocational Behavior, 67(3), 459-475. doi:10.1016/j.jvb.2004.09.004

Paglis, L. L., Green, S. G., & Bauer, T. N. (2006). Does advisor mentoring add value? A longitudinal study of mentoring and doctoral students outcomes. Research in Higher Education, 47(4), 451-476. Retrieved from doi.org/10.1007/s11162-005-9003-2

Passmore, J., Peterson, D. B., & Freire, T. (2013). The Wiley-Blackwell handbook of the psychology of coaching and mentoring. Malden, MA: John Wiley & Sons.

Patton, M. (1990). Qualitative evaluation and research methods. London: Sage. Patton, M. (2001). Qualitative research and evaluation methods (3rd ed.). Thousand Oaks, CA: Sage.

Pena, E. V., West, I. J., Gokalp, G., Fischer, L., & Gupton, J. (2011). Exploring effective support practices for doctoral students' degree completion. College Student Journal, 45(2), 310-317. Retrieved from projectinnovation.biz/home

Petersen, R., Eggert, A., Grümmer, R., Schara, U., & Sauerwein, W. (2012). The mentoring of women for medical career development. International Journal of Mentoring and Coaching in Education, 1(2), 155-168 dx.doi.org/10.1108/20466851211262888

Phipps, A. (2011). Preparing adolescents for bariatric surgery: Foundational elements applying Erikson's theory of human development. Bariatric Nursing and Surgical Patient Care, 6(4), 179-184. dx.doi.org/10.1089/bar.2011.9947

Pollock, R. (1995). A test of conceptual models depicting the developmental course of informal mentor–protégé relationships in the workplace. Journal of Vocational Behavior, 46, 144–162. Retrieved from doi.org/10.1006/jvbe.1995.1010

Pomeroy, E. C., & Steiker, L. H. (2011). Paying it forward: On mentors and mentoring. Social Work, 56(3), 197-199. Retrieved from doi.org/10.1093/sw/56.3.197

Popoola, F., Adesopo, A., & Ajayi, M. (2013). Establishing effective mentoring culture among professional university administrators in Nigeria. Public Administration Research, 2(2), 134-147. Retrieved from doi.org/10.5539/par.v2n2p134

Poronsky, C. B. (2012). A literature review of mentoring for RN-to-FNP transition. Journal of Nursing Education, 51(11), 623-31. Retrieved from: dx.doi.org/10.3928/01484834-20120914-03

Prevodnik, M., & Biloslavo, R. (2009). Managers and leaders in organizations of a post-transition economy. Organizacija, 42(3), 87. Retrieved from: dx.doi.org/10.2478/v10051-009-0006-1

Price, A., & McMullan, L. (2012). We don't need no education: The role of mentoring in the wider enterprise eco-system. International Journal of Gender and Entrepreneurship, 4(2), 196-205. Retrieved from: dx.doi.org/10.1108/17566261211234670

Pryce, J. (2012). Mentor attunement: An approach to successful school-based mentoring relationships. Child & Adolescent Social Work Journal, 29(4), 285-305. dx.doi.org/10.1007/s10560-012-0260-6

Pyhalto, K. & Keskinen, J. (2012). Doctoral students' sense of relational agency in their scholarly communities. International Journal of Higher Education, 1(2), 136-149. Retrieved from doi.org/10.5430/ijhe.v1n2p136

Ragins, B. R. & Kram, K. E. (2007). The roots and meaning of mentoring. Thousand Oaks, CA: Sage.

Ragins, B. R. & Kram, K. E. (2009). The handbook of mentoring at work: Theory, research, and practice. Thousand Oaks, CA: Sage. doi: http://dx.doi.org/10.4135/9781412976619

Rausch, J. L. (2012). A case study of the identity development of an adolescent male with emotional disturbance and 48, XYYY karyotype in an institutional setting. The Qualitative Report, 17(1), 222-243. Retrieved from http://tqr.nova.edu/

Rayford, S. (2014). A qualitative analysis of mentoring experiences and perceptions of female students enrolled in a doctoral program in education at a Midwestern University (Doctoral dissertation). Retrieved from ProQuest database. (Accession No. 3728016)

Reddick, R. J. (2012). Male faculty mentors in black and white. International Journal of Mentoring and Coaching in Education, 1(1), 36-53. dx.doi.org/10.1108/20466851211231611

Reinstein, A., Sinason, D. H., & Fogarty, T. J. (2012). Examining mentoring in public accounting organizations. Review of Business, 33(1), 40-49. Retrieved from stjohns.edu/

Rekha, K. N., & Ganesh, M. P. (2012). Do mentors learn by mentoring others? International Journal of Mentoring and Coaching in Education, 1(3), 205-217. dx.doi.org/10.1108/20466851211279466

Rhodes, J. E., Grossman, J. B., & Resch, N. R. (2000). Agents of change: Pathways through which mentoring relationships influence adolescents' academic adjustments. Child Development, 71, 1662-1671. Retrieved from doi.org/10.1111/1467-8624.00256

Rhodes, J. E., Spencer, R., Keller, T. E., Liang, B., & Noam, G. (2006). A model for the influence of mentoring relationships on youth development. Journal of Community Psychology, 34(6), 691-707. Retrieved from doi.org/10.1002/jcop.20124

Ricks, J. J. (2013). Collaborating partners: An effective mentoring program for school libraries. Knowledge Quest, 41(4), 16-21. Retrieved from ala.org

Rigg, J., Day, J., & Adler, H. (2013). Emotional exhaustion in graduate students: The role of engagement, self-efficacy and social support. Journal of Educational and Developmental Psychology, 3(2), 138-152. Retrieved from doi.org/10.5539/jedp.v3n2p138

Robinson, D. M., & Reio, T. G., Jr. (2012). Benefits of mentoring African-American men. Journal of Managerial Psychology, 27(4), 406-421. dx.doi.org/10.1108/02683941211220207

Rowan, M., & Huston, P. (1997). Qualitative research articles: Information for authors and peer reviews. Canadian Medical Association Journal, 157(10), 1442-6. Retrieved from cmaj.ca/

Rubin, K. H. (1998). Social and emotional development from a cultural perspective. Developmental Psychology, 34(4), 611-615. dx.doi.org/10.1037/0012-1649.34.4.611

Rueywei, G., Shih-Ying, C., & Shin-Lung, L. (2011). Does mentoring work? The Mediating effect of mentoring in China. Social Behavior & Personality: An International Journal, 39(6), 807-824. doi:10.2224/sbp.2011.39.6.807

Rusbult, C. E., Martz, J. M., & Agnew, C. R. (1998). The investment model scale: Measuring commitment level, satisfaction level, quality of alternatives, and investment size. Personal Relationships, 5(4), 357-391. doi:10.1111/j.1475- 6811.1998.tb00177.x

Russell, G. M., & Horne, S. G. (2009). Finding equilibrium: Mentoring, sexual orientation, and gender identity. Professional Psychology: Research and Practice, 40(2), 194-200. dx.doi.org/10.1037/a0011860

Rutti, R. M., Helms, M. M., & Rose, L. C. (2013). Changing the lens. Leadership & Organization Development Journal, 34(5), 446-468. dx.doi.org/10.1108/LODJ-11-0097

Saade, R. G. & Kira, D. (2007). Mediating the impact of technology usage on perceived ease of use by anxiety. Computers & Education, 49, 1189-1204. doi: 10.101 6/j.compedu.2006.01.009

Sabie, O., & Androniceanu, A. (2012). Persuasive communication at the academic level and how to make it more effective. Administratie Si Management Public, (18), 26-52. Retrieved from http://miar.ub.edu/issn/1583-9583

Sanfey, H., Hollands, C., & Gantt, N. L. (2013). Strategies for building an effective mentoring relationship. The American Journal of Surgery, 206(5), 714-718. dx.doi.org/10.1016/j.amjsurg.2013.08.001

Santora, K. A., Mason, E. J., & Sheahan, T. C. (2013). A model for progressive mentoring in science and engineering education and research. Innovative Higher Education, 38(5), 427-440. dx.doi.org/10.1007/s10755-013-9255-2

Sarri, K. K. (2011). Mentoring female entrepreneurs: A mentors' training intervention evaluation. Journal of European Industrial Training, 35(7), 721-741. dx.doi.org/10.1108/03090591111160814

Scandura, T.A., & Ragins, B. R. (1993). The effects of sex and gender role orientation on mentorship in male-dominated occupations. *Journal of Vocational Behavior, 43,* 251–265. Retrieved from doi.org/10.1006/jvbe.1993.1046

Schempp, P. (1987). Research on teaching in physical education: Beyond the limits of the natural science. *Journal of Teaching in Physical Education, 6,* 111-121. Retrieved from doi.org/10.1123/jtpe.6.2.111

Schmidt, D., Robinson, K., & Webster, E. (2014). Factors influencing attrition from a researcher training program. *International Journal for Researcher Development,5*(1), 56-67. dx.doi.org/10.1108/IJRD-08-2013-0013

Schulze, S. (2014). Finding the academic self: Identity development of academics as doctoral students. *Koers, 79*(1), 1-8. Retrieved from doi.org/10.4102/koers.v79i1.2114

Schunk, D. H., & Mullen, C. A. (2013). Toward a conceptual model of mentoring research: Integration with self-regulated learning. *Educational Psychology Review, 25*(3), 361-389. dx.doi.org/10.1007/s10648-013-9233-3

Schutte, N. S., Malouff, J. M., & Thorsteinsson, E. B. (2013). Increasing emotional intelligence through training: Current status and future directions. *International Journal of Emotional Education, 5*(1), 56-72. Retrieved from https://www.um.edu.mt/ijee

Schutz, W.C. (1958). *FIRO. A three-dimensional theory of interpersonal relations.* New York, NY: Holt, Rinehart & Winston.

Shahid, A., & Azhar, S. M. (2013). Integrity & trust: The defining principles of great workplaces. *Journal of Management Research, 5*(4), 64-75. Retrieved from doi.org/10.5296/jmr.v5i4.3739

Shank, G. D. (2006). *Qualitative research: A personal skills approach* (2nd ed.). Upper Saddle River, NJ: Prentice Hall.

Shojai, S., Davis, W. J., & Root, P. S. (2014). Developmental relationship programs: An empirical study of the impact of peer-mentoring programs. *Contemporary Issues in Education Research (Online), 7*(1), 31-38. Retrieved from doi.org/10.19030/cier.v7i1.8309

Siegel, P. H., Smith, J. W., & Mosca, J. B. (2001). Mentoring relationships and interpersonal orientation. *Leadership & Organization Development Journal, 22*(3), 114-126. Retrieved from doi.org/10.1108/01437730110389265

Singh, P., & Mahomed, C. C. (2013). Exploring the collegial relationship between mentors and their mentees. *The International Business & Economics Research Journal (Online), 12*(12), 1547-1562. Retrieved from doi.org/10.19030/iber.v12i12.8249

Sinkovics, R. R., Penz, E., & Ghauri, P. N. (2008). Enhancing the trustworthiness of qualitative research in international business. *Management International Review, 48*(6), 689-713. Retrieved from doi.org/10.1007/s11575-008-0103-z

Smethem, L. (2007). Retention and intention in teaching careers: Will the new generation stay? *Teachers and Teaching, 13*(5), 465-480. Retrieved from doi.org/10.1080/13540600701561661

Smith, D. G., & Delmore, B. (2007). Three key components to successfully completing a nursing doctoral program. *The Journal of Continuing Education in Nursing,38*(2), 76-82. dx.doi.org/10.3928/00220124-20070301-01

Smith, M. V. (2005). Modern mentoring: Ancient lessons for today. *Music Educators Journal, 92*(2), 62-67. Retrieved from doi.org/10.2307/3400199

Smith, L. H., & Holloman, C. (2013). Comparing the effects of teen mentors to adult teachers on child lifestyle behaviors and health outcomes in Appalachia. *The Journal of School Nursing, 29*(5), 386-96. dx.doi.org/10.1177/1059840512472708

Stadler, M. (2012). Engines of growth: Education and innovation. *Jahrbuch Für Wirtschaftswissenschaften, 63*(2), 113-124. Retrieved from doi.org/10.1515/roe-2012-0202

Stake, R. E. (1995). *The art of case study research.* Thousand Oaks, CA: Sage. Stake, R. E. (2006). *Multiple-case study analysis.* Thousand Oaks, CA: Sage.

Stallone, M. N. (2011). Factors associated with student attrition and retention in an educational leadership doctoral program. *Journal of College Teaching & Learning, 1*(6), 17-24. Retrieved from doi.org/10.19030/tlc.v1i6.1952

Starr-Glass, D. (2013). Threshold work: Sustaining liminality in mentoring international students. *International Journal of Mentoring and Coaching in Education, 2*(2), 109-121.

Retrieved from doi.org/10.1108/IJMCE-11-2012-0073

Stein, C. H., & Mankowski, E. S. (2004). Asking, witnessing, interpreting, knowing: Conducting qualitative research in community psychology. American Journal of Community Psychology, 33(1-2), 21-35. dx.doi.org/10.1023/B:AJCP.0000014316.27091.e8

Stephens, S., Doherty, O., Bennett, B., & Margey, M. (2014). The challenge of work based learning: A role for academic mentors? International Journal of Mentoring and Coaching in Education, 3(2), 158-170. Retrieved from doi.org/10.1108/IJMCE-03-2013-0020

Stephenson, M. & Christensen, R. (2007). Mentoring for doctoral student praxis-centered learning: Creating a shared culture of intellectual aspiration. Nonprofit & Voluntary Sector Quarterly, 36(4), 64-79. Retrieved from doi.org/10.1177/0899764007305055

St-jean, E., & Audet, J. (2012). The role of mentoring in the learning development of the novice entrepreneur. International Entrepreneurship and Management Journal, 8(1), 119-140. dx.doi.org/10.1007/s11365-009-0130-7

Straus, S. E., & Sackett, D. L. (2012). Clinician-trialist rounds: 10. mentoring - part 4: Attributes of an effective mentor. Clinical Trials, 9(3), 367-369. dx.doi.org/10.1177/1740774512440343

Struthers, N. (1995). Differences in mentoring: A function of gender or organizational rank? Journal of Social Behavior and Personality, 10(6):265-272. Retrieved from sbp-journal.com/index.php/sbp

Sugimoto, C. R. (2012a). Are you my mentor? Identifying mentors and their roles in LIS doctoral education. Journal of Education for Library and Information Science, 53(1), 2-19. Retrieved from alise.org/jelis-2

Sugimoto, C. R. (2012b). Initiation, cultivation, separation and redefinition: Application of Kram's mentoring framework to doctoral education in information and library science. Journal of Education for Library and Information Science, 53(2), 98-114. Retrieved from alise.org/jelis-2

Tagreed, I. K. (2012). Cross-cultural differences in management. International Journal of Business and Social Science, 3(6). Retrieved from ijbssnet.com/

Tellis, W. (1997). Application of a case study methodology. The Qualitative Report, 3(3). Retrieved from http://tqr.nova.edu/

Terry, K. Y., DeMichiell, R., & Williams, C. (2009). Mentoring tradeoffs: Breaking into the world of academe. Proceedings of Informing Science & IT Education Conference (InSITE), 3-17. Retrieved from http://proceedings.informingscience.org/

Tice, T. N. (1996). Mentoring. The Education Digest, 62(2), 42-45. Retrieved from eddigest.com/

Toby, M. E. (2005). The impact of learning goal orientation similarity on formal mentoring relationship outcomes. Advances in Developing Human Resources, 7(4), 489-504. Retrieved from doi.org/10.1177/1523422305279679

Townsend, A., Cox, S. M., & Li, L. C. (2010). Qualitative research ethics: Enhancing evidence-based practice in physical therapy. Physical Therapy, 90(4), 615-28. Retrieved from doi.org/10.2522/ptj.20080388

Trochim, W. M. K. (2006). Qualitative validity. Retrieved from socialresearchmethods.net/kb/qualval.php

Tufford, L. & Newman, P. (2010). Bracketing in qualitative research. Qualitative Social Work, 11(1), 80-96. Retrieved from doi.org/10.1177/1473325010368316

Ugrin, J. C., Odom, M. D., & Pearson, J. M. (2008). Exploring the importance of mentoring for new scholars: A social exchange perspective. Journal of Information Systems Education, 19(3), 343-350. Retrieved from http://jise.org/

Ugrin, J. C., Odom, M. D., Pearson, J. M., & Bahmanziari, T. R. (2012). Exploring the effects of social exchange relationships on the scholarly productivity of new faculty members in accounting. American Journal of Business Education (Online), 5(4), 385-400. Retrieved from doi.org/10.19030/ajbe.v5i4.7116

University of Phoenix (2015). IRB Corner: Field Testing, Pilot Studies, and IRB Review Timing. University of Phoenix Research Center, IRB Corner. Retrieved from https://research.phoenix.edu/news/irb-corner-august-2015

U.S. Census (2010). State area measurements and internal point coordinates. Retrieved from census.gov/geo/reference/state-area.html

Utrilla, P. N., & Grande, F. A. (2012). How mentoring affects to companies and employees? The Business Review, Cambridge, 20(1), 236-242. Retrieved from jaabc.com/brc.html

van Manen, M. (1997). *Researching lived experience: Human science for an action sensitive pedagogy* (2nd ed.). London, Ontario: The Althouse Press.

Vaughns, A. B. (2013). Expanding conceptions of quality: Cultivating trusting relationships in early learning and development programs. Childhood Education, 89(5), 323-324. Retrieved from doi.org/10.1080/00094056.2013.830916

Veal, J. L., Bull, M. J., & Miller, J. F. (2012). A framework of academic persistence and success for ethnically diverse graduate nursing students. Nursing Education Perspectives, 33(5), 322-327. Retrieved from doi.org/10.5480/1536-5026-33.5.322

Vekkaila, J., Pyhältö, K., Hakkarainen, K., Keskinen, J., & Lonka, K. (2012). Doctoral students' key learning experiences in the natural sciences. International Journal for Researcher Development, 3(2), 154-183. dx.doi.org/10.1108/17597511311316991

Vekkaila, J., Pyhältö, K., & Lonka, K. (2014). Engaging and disengaging doctoral experiences in the behavioural sciences. International Journal for Researcher Development, 5(1), 33-55. dx.doi.org/10.1108/IJRD-09-2013-0015

Waddell-Terry, T. (2014). The impact of multiple mentoring relationships on attrition in the Ed.D program (Doctoral dissertation). ProQuest database. (Accession No. 3625777)

Wahat, N. W. A., Krauss, S. E., & Othman, J. (2013). Leadership development through workplace learning in Malaysian organizations. Asian Social Science, 9(5), 298-306. Retrieved from ccsenet.org/journal/index.php/ass/index

Wahyuni, D. (2012). The research design maze: Understanding paradigms, cases, methods and methodologies. Journal of Applied Management Accounting Research, 10(1), 69-80. Retrieved from emeraldinsight.com/loi/jaar

Wainwright, M. & Russell, A. (2010). Using NVivo audio-coding: Practical, sensorial and epistemological considerations. (2010). Social Research Update, (60), 1-4. Retrieved from http://sru.soc.surrey.ac.uk/

Wang, J., & Fulton, L. A. (2012). Mentor-novice relationships and learning to teach in teacher induction: A critical review of research. REMIE Multidisciplinary Journal of Educational Research, 2(1), 56-104. Retrieved from http://hipatiapress.com/hpjournals/index.php/remie/index

Wang, S., Tomlinson, E. C., & Noe, R. A. (2010). The role of mentor trust and protégé internal locus of control in formal mentoring relationships. Journal of Applied Psychology, 95(2), 358-367. dx.doi.org/10.1037/a0017663

Ware, P., & Ramos, J. (2013). First-generation college students: Mentoring through social media. International Journal of Mentoring and Coaching in Education, 2(2), 149-162. Retrieved from doi.org/10.1108/IJMCE-02-2013-0009

Washburn-Moses, L. (2010). Rethinking mentoring: Comparing policy and practice in special and general education. Education Policy Analysis Archives, 18(32), 1-21. Retrieved from http://epaa.asu.edu/ojs/

Washington, C. E. (2011). Mentoring, organizational rank, and women's perceptions of advancement opportunities in the workplace. International Journal of Business and Social Science, 2(9), 162-178. Retrieved from ijbssnet.com/

Wendy, M. M., & Kram, K. E. (2010). Understanding non-work relationships in developmental networks. Career Development International, 15(7), 637-663. dx.doi.org/10.1108/13620431011094069

Whiting, V. R., & de Janasz, S. C. (2004). Mentoring in the 21st century: Using the Internet to build skills and networks. Journal of Management Education, 28(3), 275-293. Retrieved from http://jme.sagepub.com/

Whitney, B. (2004). Mentors: Benevolent fools or goddesses of power? Critical Quarterly, 46(3), 111-115. doi:10.1111/j.0011-1562.2004.00589.x

Williams, C. L. (2012). A funny thing happened on the way to my ph.D.: Exploring issues affecting attrition and completion in the doctoral program in instructional technology at a major research university (Doctoral dissertation). Retrieved from http://scholarworks.gsu.edu/msit_diss/102/

Williams, R. & Blackburn, R. T., (1988). Mentoring and junior faculty productivity. Journal of Nursing Education, 27(5), 204-209. Retrieved from healio.com/journals/jne

Willis, J. W. (2007). Foundations of qualitative research: Interpretive and critical approaches. Thousand Oaks, CA: Sage.

Willis, B., & Carmichael, K. D. (2011). The lived experience of late-stage doctoral student attrition in counselor education. The Qualitative Report, 16(1), 192-207. Retrieved from http://tqr.nova.edu/

Wright, K. S. (1992). From the odyssey to the university: What is this thing called mentoring? Association for Communication Administration Bulletin, 79, 45-53. Retrieved from unco.edu/aca/

Wright, S. (2015). Relational agency from a teacher as researcher perspective. *Cultural Studies of Science Education, 10*(3), 629-636. doi.org/10.1007/s11422-015-9664-x

Wu, S. Y., Turban, D. B., & Cheung, Y. H. (2012). Social skill in workplace mentoring relationships. Journal of Organizational Culture, Communication and Conflict, 16(2), 51-62. Retrieved from alliedacademies.org/journal-of- organizational-culture-communications-and-conflict/

Wyman, B. M. (2012). A hermeneutic phenomenological study of non-completers in online doctor of education programs (Unpublished doctoral dissertation). Liberty University, Lynchburg, VA.

Yamauchi, L. A. (1998). Individualism, collectivism, and cultural compatibility: Implications for counselors and teachers. Journal of Humanistic Education and Development, 36(4), 189-198. Retrieved from doi.org/10.1002/j.2164- 4683.1998.tb00391.x

Yim, L., & Waters, L. (2013). The role of interpersonal comfort, attributional confidence, and communication quality in academic mentoring relationships. Education Research and Perspectives (Online), 40, 58-85. Retrieved from erpjournal.net/

Yin, R. K. (1994). Case study research: Design and methods (2nd ed.). Thousand Oaks, CA: Sage.

Yin, R. K. (2003). Case study research: Design and methods (3rd ed.). Thousand Oaks, CA: Sage.

Yin, R. K. (2009). Case study research: Design and methods (4th ed.). Thousand Oaks, CA: Sage.

Yin, R. K. (2014). Case study research: Design and methods (5th ed.). Thousand Oaks, CA: Sage.

Yob, I., & Crawford, L. (2012). Conceptual framework for mentoring doctoral students. Higher Learning Research Communications, 2(2), 34-47. Retrieved from doi.org/10.18870/hlrc.v2i2.66

Zinko, R., Gentry, W. A., Hall, A., & Grant, G. L. (2012). Reputational change among managers. Journal of Managerial Issues, 24(1), 9-26. Retrieved from https://www.questia.com/library/p4318/journal-of-managerial-issues

Zipp, G. P., Cahill, T., & Clark, M. (2009). The role of collaborative scholarship in the mentorship of doctoral students. Journal of College Teaching and Learning, 6(8), 29-35. Retrieved from cluteinstitute.com/

Zozakiewicz, C. (2010). Culturally responsible mentoring: Exploring the impact of an alternative approach for repairing student teachers for diversity. The Teacher Educator, 45(2), 137-151. Retrieved from doi.org/10.1080/08878731003628585

INDEX

academic deans 19, 91, 111, 167
academic domain 83
academic goals ... 18, 47, 69, 71, 72, 159, 160, 211
academic institution ... 36, 69, 88, 117, 155, 166, 181, 185
academic institutions . 11, 15, 17, 18, 28, 35, 43, 50, 53, 54, 56, 57, 58, 62, 63, 65, 67, 70, 78, 88, 108, 118, 155, 158, 161, 162, 165, 168, 169, 181, 185
academic leaders 21, 41, 50, 55, 59, 166, 167, 169
academic learning 71
academic performance 30
academic studies 48
academic writing 15
advisor 42, 73, 89, 126, 129, 136, 140, 199
affection 29
African-American 87, 120, 200
anonymity 37, 97, 99, 117
Athena, the Goddess of Wisdom 41
attrition rate 11, 18, 68, 79
attrition rates .. 11, 18, 19, 30, 66, 80, 150, 162, 166, 167, 191
audio recording 37, 99
barriers 57, 65, 189, 190, 197
behaviors 21, 47, 83, 92, 104, 193, 201
biological maturation 49
bond 42, 45, 52
boundaries 32, 37, 64, 81
bracketing 37, 106, 107
brick and mortar schools 63

business leaders 20, 24
business manager leaders 20, 21
career success 17
case findings 25
challenges 17, 28, 55, 57, 59, 64, 66, 70, 73, 83, 84, 88, 156, 158, 161, 168, 169, 189, 194
characteristics 28, 30, 59, 60, 72, 76, 83, 85, 89, 92, 162, 195
coach 17, 73, 195
coding 26, 37, 108, 110, 118, 193, 203
cognitive development 12, 27, 28, 33, 44, 49, 50, 96, 101, 102, 107, 112, 114, 115, 121, 122, 123, 124, 125, 133, 134, 154, 155, 157, 164, 166, 183, 187, 188, 192
colleague 46
communication skills 30, 74
community leaders 22
compatibility ... 11, 15, 16, 19, 20, 23, 24, 25, 27, 28, 29, 35, 38, 41, 61, 83, 85, 86, 87, 88, 89, 91, 92, 93, 94, 95, 100, 102, 104, 108, 109, 111, 116, 121, 126, 128, 129, 135, 144, 147, 150, 153, 154, 160, 163, 164, 165, 166, 168, 169, 170, 173, 177, 181, 183, 185, 188, 204
competence ... 16, 31, 48, 49, 56, 70, 71, 83, 86
confidence 33, 37, 49, 51, 60, 70, 79, 105, 134, 160, 181, 185, 198, 204
confidentiality ... 37, 99, 118, 131,

181, 185
consequences 18, 190, 192, 195
constructive opinions 21
control 29, 71, 146, 190, 203, 215
credentials 73, 142
cross-case analysis . 11, 26, 108, 110, 121
cultivation 28, 31, 44, 45, 51, 202
cultivation phase 45, 51
cultural backgrounds . 15, 18, 30, 78
cultural compatibility 30
cultural differences .. 18, 78, 165, 170, 202
Culture 77, 204
data analysis 11, 26, 37, 103, 108, 110, 116, 120, 150, 153, 164, 170, 193
delimitations 37, 163
delivery style 62
demographic 119, 162
developmental stages 16, 46
disciplinary cultures 18
disposition 33, 214, 217
dissertation 3, 13, 34, 50, 53, 79, 83, 89, 115, 122, 123, 124, 125, 126, 127, 129, 139, 155, 166, 190, 200, 203, 204
dissertation research 34, 50
dissertations 19, 75
doctoral chairs 15, 17, 19, 91, 111, 167
doctoral mentors .. 16, 19, 22, 23, 24, 25, 26, 27, 32, 33, 35, 38, 41, 44, 84, 85, 91, 93, 103, 109, 111, 116, 118, 150, 153, 159, 162, 163, 164, 167, 169, 170
doctoral programs 11, 15, 16, 17, 18, 19, 20, 24, 27, 33, 38, 41, 44, 51, 52, 55, 60, 61, 62, 63, 65, 68, 71, 72, 73, 80, 82, 85, 86, 88, 89, 91, 94, 95, 98, 100, 104, 109, 111, 116, 121, 141, 144, 145, 150, 153, 154, 160, 163, 164, 166, 167, 169, 170, 173, 174, 177, 181, 185, 192
doctoral students . 11, 15, 16, 17, 18, 19, 21, 22, 23, 24, 27, 30, 31, 33, 35, 38, 43, 46, 47, 48, 50, 51, 52, 55, 56, 57, 61, 62, 63, 64, 65, 66, 67, 68, 69, 70, 71, 72, 75, 78, 79, 80, 81, 82, 83, 84, 85, 86, 87, 88, 89, 93, 95, 97, 101, 102, 104, 111, 112, 113, 114, 119,120, 122, 126, 133, 140, 144, 145, 146, 150, 155, 156, 157, 158, 161, 167, 168, 169, 170, 183, 188, 191, 192, 193, 194, 195, 199, 201, 204
Doctorate of Education See Ed.D.
dropouts 80
Eagle University 79
Ed.D. .... See Doctorate of Education, See Doctorate of Education, See Doctorate of Education, See Doctorate of Education, See Doctorate of Education
educators 22
EI See Emotional Intelligence
Emotional Intelligence ...... See EI
emotional stability 49, 50
emotional state 75
emotions ... 29, 37, 48, 69, 74, 76
Encyclopedia of Children's Health 49, 192
enrollments 19
environmental experiences 49
environmental influences 28
ethnographic research study .. 93
expectations .. 15, 17, 28, 44, 51, 57, 58, 59, 69, 74, 78, 79, 88, 131, 143, 156, 160, 161, 162
face-to-face mentoring 52, 64
faculty members .. 17, 43, 64, 84, 87, 149, 194, 202
feedback 53, 55, 58, 98, 103, 112, 113, 116, 127, 142, 149,

157, 168, 173, 185
field experts 113
field test ... 23, 98, 103, 104, 105, 112, 113, 116, 173, 174, 175, 185
FIRO- B 29
formal mentoring process 28
formal mentoring program 84
friend 41, 46
geographical barriers.............. 65
Goodness of Fit 44
grounded theory 94, 193, 196
higher education leaders 20
honesty............................ 36, 60
human factors........................ 82
Human Resource Development 87, 193
hypotheses 24, 94
identity development . 28, 33, 44, 46, 48, 199
inclusion 29, 190
incompatibility 19, 29, 30
inequality 32
influence .. 12, 21, 29, 36, 44, 49, 52, 55, 61, 74, 102, 106, 115, 121, 122, 128, 133, 134, 135, 158, 159, 169, 183, 187, 188, 194, 195, 196, 200
influences 29, 49, 53, 88, 89, 157, 196
Informed Consent Letter......... 99
initiation ... 27, 28, 31, 44, 51, 95, 101, 107, 111, 114, 130, 154, 156, 161, 164, 165, 183, 187
initiation phase 31, 51, 114, 156, 161
initiatives.................. 67, 161, 168
interpersonal confidence 30
Interpersonal relationship 34
interpersonal relationship skills48
interpersonal relationships16, 48, 61, 89, 197
interpersonal traits 30
interview questions.... 11, 23, 24, 25, 27, 35, 36, 37, 38, 95, 98,

99, 100, 101, 102, 103, 104, 112, 113, 117, 121, 141, 151, 154, 173, 185
interviews 11, 23, 24, 25, 26, 92, 98, 100, 101, 104, 106, 107, 108, 111, 112, 116, 117, 120, 122, 174, 178
Kram, Kathy... 28, 31, 32, 38, 42, 44, 45, 46, 51, 52, 54, 57, 156, 158, 159, 161, 196, 199, 202, 203
leader 22, 73, 192, 220
Leader Member Exchange ... See LMX
leaders12, 21, 41, 64, 73, 76, 88, 111, 153, 167, 168, 199, 213, 219
leadership 17, 21, 22, 30, 36, 73, 76, 78, 127, 136, 138, 140, 151, 153, 164, 166, 167, 168, 191, 193, 196, 197, 198, 201
Leadership development 34, 203
leadership roles 21
learning conditions 15
learning needs........ 21, 111, 167
Levinson, David .. 42, 50, 52, 196
lines of inquiry 83
LMX ....See Leader Member Exchange, See Leader Member Exchange, See Leader Member Exchange, See Leader Member Exchange, See Leader Member Exchange
management 21, 22, 58, 190, 196, 202, 213, 215, 216, 220
matching process .. 12, 102, 115, 121, 126, 128, 130, 135, 155, 158, 162, 165, 168, 183, 188
maturity levels 49
measurement tool................... 61
mental attitudes 30, 48
mentee15, 16, 18, 21, 25, 27, 28, 31, 34, 38, 43, 45, 46, 49, 50, 51, 53, 54, 58, 59, 60, 64, 73,

74, 76, 80, 87, 89, 96, 101, 112, 114, 115, 123, 134, 146, 154, 157, 160, 161, 164, 165, 170, 183, 187, 188, 189, 190, 192, 196, 198
mentees
   protégés 15, 16, 17, 18, 19, 21, 22, 27, 28, 29, 30, 31, 32, 33, 38, 39, 41, 42, 43, 44, 45, 46, 47, 48, 49, 50, 51, 52, 53, 54, 55, 56, 57, 58, 59, 60, 61, 62, 63, 64, 65, 66, 69, 70, 71, 72, 73, 74, 75, 76, 77, 78, 83, 84, 88, 93, 96, 97, 101, 102, 114, 115, 116, 136, 137, 146, 148, 155, 156, 157, 158, 159, 160, 161, 162, 164, 165, 166, 167, 170, 183, 187, 188, 195, 201
mentor programs 21
Mentor Relationship 34, 54
mentor training system 78
mentor/mentee 11, 16, 19, 20, 25, 27, 43, 50, 82, 87, 95, 96, 101, 102, 111, 112, 114, 115, 122, 123, 125, 141, 150, 154, 161, 162, 164, 165, 166, 168, 170, 183, 187, 188
mentor/mentee relationship ... 16, 20, 27, 82, 95, 96, 101, 102, 111, 112, 114, 123, 125, 141, 154, 161, 164, 183, 187
mentoring 11, 12, 15, 16, 17, 18, 19, 20, 21, 22, 23, 24, 25, 27, 28, 29, 30, 31, 32, 33, 35, 38, 41, 42, 43, 44, 45, 46, 47, 48, 49, 50, 51, 52, 53, 54, 55, 56, 57, 58, 59, 60, 61, 62, 63, 64, 65, 66, 67, 68, 70, 71, 72, 73, 74, 75, 76, 77, 78, 79, 80, 82, 83, 84,85, 86, 87, 88, 89, 91, 92, 93, 94, 95, 96, 97, 100, 101, 102, 103, 104, 107, 109, 111, 112, 113, 114, 115, 116, 118, 119, 121, 130, 141, 142, 144, 145, 146, 147, 149, 150, 153, 154, 156, 157, 158, 159,
160, 161, 162, 163, 164, 165, 166, 167, 168, 169, 170, 173, 174, 177, 181, 183, 185, 187, 188, 189, 190, 191, 192, 193, 194, 195, 196, 197, 198, 199, 200, 201, 202, 203, 204, 219, 221
Mentoring at Work 42
mentoring cycle 28, 45, 52
mentoring deficiencies 53
mentoring models 28, 44
mentoring practices 22, 167
mentoring process 11, 17, 19, 20, 35, 67, 68, 70, 74, 89, 158, 167, 168, 169, 170
mentoring programs .. 17, 50, 55, 60, 64, 70, 78, 84, 88, 89, 91, 166
mentoring relationship 17, 23, 28, 29, 31, 32, 35, 38, 39, 41, 44, 48, 51, 52, 53, 54, 56, 58, 59, 60, 61, 62, 63, 65, 66, 67, 68, 71, 72, 74, 75, 76, 79, 80, 83, 84, 85, 88, 94, 95, 97, 114, 141, 156, 159, 160, 166, 167, 168, 170
Mentoring relationships ... 15, 16, 17, 18, 20, 21, 22, 29, 36, 38, 39, 44, 45, 51, 52, 54, 55, 56, 57, 60, 61, 63, 67, 68, 74, 78, 84, 85, 87, 88, 89, 93, 94, 95, 97, 153, 154, 157, 160, 161, 167, 169, 170, 181, 198, 201
mentors ... 11, 12, 15, 16, 17, 18, 19, 20, 21, 22, 23, 24, 25, 26, 27, 28, 29, 30, 31, 32, 33, 34, 35, 37, 38, 41, 42, 43, 44, 45, 46, 48, 49, 50, 51, 52, 53, 54, 55, 56, 57, 58, 59, 60, 61, 62, 63, 64, 65, 66, 68, 69, 70, 71, 72, 73, 74, 75, 76, 77, 78, 83, 84, 85,88, 89, 91, 93, 94, 95, 96, 97, 100, 101, 102, 103, 104, 108, 109, 111, 112, 113, 114, 115, 116, 118, 119, 120,

126, 128, 131, 135, 136, 138, 146, 147, 148, 149, 150, 153, 154, 155, 156, 157, 158, 159, 160, 161, 162, 163, 164, 165, 166, 167, 168, 169, 170,173, 177, 183, 185, 188, 190, 191, 194, 195, 196, 197, 198, 199, 200, 201, 202, 203
mentors' perceptions 38, 85
mentorship practices 21, 96, 111, 167
mentorship relationship 11, 38
Mentorship training 79
models of mentoring 28
moral composition 30, 76
motivation 13, 14, 74, 75, 84, 161, 194, 211
motivational skills 30
mutual engagement 44
networking 12, 121, 135, 136, 137, 158, 165, 170
non-traditional education 29
non-traditional mentoring 29
NVivo 11, 26, 106, 108, 109, 120, 121, 153, 170, 198, 203
NVivo11 .... 26, 108, 110
obligations 54, 69
obstacles 30, 53, 57
Odysseus 41
online classes 29, 63, 64, 65
online education 62, 189, 197
online environment 62, 64, 65, 83
online program 63, 81
openness 36
Organizational management .. 22
orientation 29, 132, 149, 162, 190, 200, 201, 202
parent (figure) 56
participants 11, 20, 22, 23, 25, 26, 27, 35, 36, 37, 38, 80, 91, 92, 93, 94, 95, 96, 97, 98, 99, 100, 103, 104, 106, 107, 108, 109, 110, 112, 113, 114, 115, 116, 117, 118, 119, 120, 125, 126, 130, 132, 135, 138, 141, 144, 147, 150, 153, 154, 155, 158, 160, 163, 164, 165, 168, 170
patterns ... 11, 24, 25, 26, 33, 93, 95, 101, 102, 108, 109, 110, 112, 114, 115, 117, 120, 150, 154, 183, 187
pedagogical needs 72
peer 46, 52, 84, 158, 200, 201
perceptions 11, 12, 19, 20, 23, 24, 25, 27, 35, 36, 37, 38, 41, 69, 82, 83, 85, 86, 87, 89, 91, 92, 93, 94, 95, 97, 100, 104, 106, 108, 109, 111, 121, 144, 147, 150, 153, 154, 160, 163, 164, 165, 166, 169, 170, 177, 190, 192, 193, 200, 203
phenomenological study .. 79, 80, 94, 204
Piaget 49, 189, 190, 192, 198
policy changes 21
population 18, 35, 89, 96, 109, 140, 163, 169
power 29, 61, 148, 191, 195, 203
problem solving 22
procedural changes 21
professional relationship 43
prospective mentors 20
protégés .. 15, 22, 42, 52, 53, 75, 77, 199
provosts 19, 91, 111, 167
psychosocial .. 16, 42, 46, 51, 54, 72, 83, 159, 160
psychosocial development 16
psychosocial domains 17
purpose statement 27, 95
purposeful sampling 23, 96, 109, 163
qualitative data 24, 26, 109, 111, 121
qualitative research ... 11, 20, 23, 24, 26, 27, 35, 92, 93, 94, 95, 96, 100, 103, 105, 106, 107, 108, 109, 112, 191, 192, 193, 195, 198, 201, 202, 204

qualitative research study 11, 20, 24, 27, 35, 93, 95, 96, 100
quantitative research 24, 92, 105, 107, 169
redefinition 28, 44, 46, 51, 202
relationship building 29, 89
reliability .. 23, 98, 103, 105, 112, 192
reputation 2, 30, 77
research abilities 15
research problem 23
research questions ... 23, 92, 104
researcher bias....................... 37
review of literature 41, 89
role model............................... 33
role-modeling.......................... 50
safe haven.............................. 61
saturation .. 12, 26, 109, 121, 198
School performance 70
self-awareness 48, 49, 73
self-efficacy 30, 74, 75, 159, 196, 200
sense of belonging 29, 198
separation 28, 31, 32, 44, 45, 51, 161, 202
share experiences 21
social characteristics 32
social factors 46
social interactions............. 49, 71
social media 2
social skills............................. 56
social-emotional development 28, 44, 47

socialization process 46
sports coaches 22
stress 15, 17, 30, 61, 69, 197
subjective data 23
superiority.............................. 32
support system 57, 66, 82
teacher 42, 73, 189, 190, 191, 194, 196, 203, 204, 211
The Odyssey 41
The Seasons of a Man's Life .. 42
themes..... 11, 24, 25, 26, 93, 95, 101, 102, 108, 109, 110, 112, 117, 120, 121, 122, 150, 153, 154, 164, 165, 170
Theoretical frameworks ... 27, 28, 88, 94
theory and model of mentoring 44
time management................... 36
traits..................... 28, 30, 72, 73
transformation 73
triangulation......................... 107
trust.... 19, 28, 34, 42, 59, 60, 74, 76, 84, 130, 141, 142, 156, 160, 194, 201, 203
trustworthiness .. 23, 48, 97, 105, 106, 191, 201
underachieving 30
University of Delaware . 100, 181
validity . 20, 23, 89, 98, 103, 105, 106, 107, 112, 202, 216, 217
variables 24, 92
video conferencing 65
Wilmington University... 100, 181

CURRICULUM VITAE

Kenneth C. Jackson, D.M.
Wilmington, DE 19804
Kennethj42867@msn.com
www.linkedin.com/in/kennethcjackson

Teaching Philosophy

Being an educator means I mentor students and assist them in reaching their personal, professional, and academic goals. The opportunity to enhance someone's learning ability and have a positive effect on their future in very motivating. As a teacher, I am hoping to leave a legacy on the world by providing support, mentorship, and instructional guidance. I provide students the necessary tools to be productive in their lives. In the classroom, I learn and grow with my students. I become a lifelong learner for the subjects I teach. Education takes on an epistemological position because there is no one, clear universal explanation of how each one of us acquires knowledge.

Knowledge is not only acquired in the classroom, but is acquired through social experiences. Past philosophers stated our sources of knowledge come from six different elements: (1) perception, (2) memory, (3) testimony, (4) introspection, (5) reasoning, and (6) rational insight. The epistemological analysis of a student's experience can indicate these sources of knowledge help shape and form the person they will become academically and professionally. It is this foundation for learning that drives me to continually improve my efforts in the classroom. I believe everyone can learn something new daily, and new knowledge gives us the tools to be more prepared in our personal, professional, and academic environment.

My primary objective in the classroom is to communicate effectively to engage students. Non-engaged students have less motivation to learn. This approach brings concepts to life and creates a connection between the instructor, student, and the topic. This approach allows me to develop collaborative projects to deepen a student's understanding.

To enhance course outcomes, it is essential to recognize students learn in different ways. Instructors must have the ability to instruct with a variety of approaches to reach each student, including discussions, case studies, simulations, or group projects. I apply a solid methodology of applying critical thinking to the activities I create to inspire deeper learning to prepare students to be successful thinkers and focuses students on their self-reported short- and long-term goals. This illustrates the importance of motivating one's self and demonstrates to students the payoff for persistence.

I keep students focused by making the learning environment unpredictable. Students become disengaged when presented too much structure in the classroom daily. To keep them focused, I incorporate a variety of learning techniques and methodologies to keep them immersed in the learning process. My goal is to become an inspiring college instructor and to meet the needs of every student, while facilitating the importance of critical thinking.

Formal Education

- 2016, Doctor of Management, Organizational Leadership, University of Phoenix, Phoenix, AZ
- 2012, Master of Health Service Administration, Strayer University, Herndon, VA
- 2011, Master of Education, Educational Management, Strayer University, Herndon, VA
- 2008, Master of Business Administration, Management, Strayer University, Herndon, VA
- 2007, Bachelor of Business Administration, Strayer University, Herndon, VA
- 2005, Associates in Arts, Business Administration, Strayer University, Herndon, VA

Teaching Experience

2017 – present, Adjunct Instructor
Montana State University Billings, Billings, MT

- Providing instruction, support, and services to students in learning Business Logistics.
- Providing personal and professional background experiences and using them as an example to teach students.
- Ensuring retention and success of students by providing them effective learning outcomes.

2017 – present, Adjunct Instructor
DeVry University, New York, NY

- Providing instruction, support, and services to students in the Keller Graduate Program of Business Management.
- Providing personal and professional background experiences and using them as an example to teach students.
- Ensuring retention and success of students by providing them effective learning outcomes.

2011 – 2012, Academic Tutor
Strayer University, Newark, DE

- Performed tutoring over 400 students in various academic subjects in: Accounting, Business Management, Leadership, APA writing, Organizational Management, Marketing
- Planned, wrote, and developed a study skills workshop and provided tips on APA writing and navigating through ICAMPUS website.
- Served as member of the Student Advisory Board.

1992 – 2006, Military Trainer
United States Navy, Norfolk, VA

- Taught junior enlistees on how to conduct business through supply chain management.
- Educated junior enlistees on how to become effective leaders.

- Instructed new personnel on various business operating procedures.

Professional Experience

2017 – Present, Procurement, Leasing, & Fleet Manager
Cecil County Government, Elkton, MD

- Responsible for managing and training two personnel for the county's procurement functions adding analytical reviews to complex purchasing requirements.
- Manages the Motor Vehicle Fund including the acquisition, disposition, and maintenance of >300 automobiles, trucks, and buses as well as heavy and mobile equipment.
- Responsible for managing Motor Vehicle and equipment inventory ensuring all vehicles are accounted for and standard operating procedures are followed for the use of such vehicles and equipment.
- Manage and oversees Property Management Fund that includes seven tenants renting county real estate.
- Manage and review department's procurement requirements for goods and services ensuring best practices are used while investigating cost saving opportunities and quality improvement.

2008 – 2017, Supply Chain Manager, V-22 Program
The Boeing Company, Ridley Park, PA

- Responsible for managing and training personnel for logistics, financial accountability, inventory, and material procurement support for V-22 Performance Based Logistics (PBL) program.

- Supervised personnel in V-22 EMD program replenishment activity and met material availability rate of 85% or higher.
- Spearheaded the creation of the V-22 PBL warehouse in Havelock NC ensuring all warehouse personnel were trained for all warehouse operations.
- Played key role in acquiring a second V-22 PBL warehouse in Greensboro NC for material overflow from Havelock NC warehouse.

- Managed and trained warehouse personnel under V-22 PBL Program for the receipt, storage, and issuing of spare parts to sustain manufacturing and production activities.
- Facilitated inventory management and warehouse inventory schedules resulting in a 100% inventory accuracy rate for 5 years.
- Maintained synchronization of the supply chain between international or domestic organizations, customers, and suppliers by utilizing Supply Chain Management (SCM) systems to support global markets.
- Planned, wrote, and established all standard desktop procedures for V-22 PBL Program, ensuring all Defense Logistics Agency requirements were 100% supported.
- Coordinated activities to support provisioning and V-22 program product deliverables.
- Developed and controlled inventory plans and integrates company, customer, and supplier capabilities to optimize inventory levels, turn rates and unit cost while ensuring accurate requirements and delivery schedules.
- Forecasted post-production supply chain support demand and maintain accurate inventory control of assets.
- Investigated feasibility of repair/overhaul and coordinates the movement of assets and components through the repair cycle.
- Identified Supply Chain alternatives to resolve obsolescence issues.

2006 – 2008, Supply Chain Manager
Corpus Christi Army Depot (CCAD)
The Boeing Company, Ridley Park, PA

- Supervised and trained personnel for logistics, financial accountability, inventory, and material procurement support for CCAD program.
- Supported the Sustainment Program ensuring over 1,500 customer demands were filled to schedule and warehouse inventory levels were maintained at target stock levels.
- Analyzed material requirements to determine appropriate attributes to drive accurate demand through the supply chain.
- Solved daily supply chain problems applying best practices to optimize efficiencies.

- Collaborated with a variety of internal and external customers and utilized forecasting/planning systems to conduct strategic and tactical management.

Military Experience

2003 – 2006, Logistics Officer (Logistics Specialist/E-7)
United States Navy, NROTC Norfolk, Norfolk, VA

- Responsible for the allocated commands budget accounts totaling over $500K meeting the needs of over 350 staff and student personnel at three major universities.
- Expertly managed and trained personnel in the organizations' clothing budget totaling over $150K with zero deficiencies.
- Maintained detailed monthly reporting procedures providing immediate knowledge of all requisition status, ensuring all supplies were received on time or ahead of schedule.
- Maintained 100% inventory validity rate of over 5,000 student textbooks and 8,000 uniform items.

1999 – 2003, Supply Division Officer (Storekeeper/E-7)
United States Navy, USS Winston S. Churchill DDG -81, Norfolk, VA

- Managed and trained 12 personnel for logistics, financial accountability, inventory, and material procurement support for seven departments.
- Oversaw the procurement of over 500,000 line items, ensuring fast receipt to meet the ship's operational commitments.
- Successfully administered the ship's $1.2M repair and consumables budget with zero discrepancies.
- Directed inventory and tracking of over 300 Depot Level Repairable repair parts totaling over $10M with zero inventory discrepancies and zero carcass charges.

1996 – 1999, Material Support Center Supervisor (Storekeeper/E-6)
United States Navy, Shore Intermediate Maintenance Activity, Norfolk, VA

- Responsible for oversight and training for 21 personnel for the inventory and material support of 19 Regional Repair Centers.

- Effectively managed requisitioning of over 500,000 material requirements.
- Produced a material receipt rate greater than 99% during demanding ships' overhaul schedules.
- Managed the expediting of over 2,000 emergent material requirements monthly, ensuring timely receipt of all repair parts and supplies.
- Supervised personnel in the material requirements processing over $25M with four work centers covering over 120 Atlantic Fleet ships that needed repair.
- Planned, wrote, and established all standard operating procedures for Regional Maintenance Material Support Center, ensuring all Regional Repair Centers were supported 100%.

1992 – 1996, Financial/Inventory Manager (Storekeeper/E-5)
United States Navy, USS Tortuga LSD 46, Norfolk, VA

- Managed and trained eight personnel at the Integrated Logistics Overhaul site, inventorying >17,000 repair parts and instrumental in disposition of >10,000 excess parts.
- Responsible for a 99.2% inventory validity for over 13,000 repair parts earning scores of 97.5% in accountability and 96.9% in sustainability (October 1995 Logistics Management Assessment).
- Tracked 300 Depot Level Repairable parts valued at $1.3M with zero inventory discrepancies and all areas remained 100% on hand/on order.
- Conducted various monthly inventory reports, ensuring storerooms had 100% on hand/on order status.

Educational Training

- 2012, eCampus Training
- 2003, Blackboard Training

Business and Technical Training and Certifications

- 2017, Introduction to Public Procurement, NIGP: The Institute for Public Procurement
- 2017, Lean Six Sigma White Belt Certified, Management and Strategy Institute
- 2011, Transition to Management Training, The Boeing Company
- 2001, Supply Financial Management, United States Navy
- 2001, Joint Aviation Supply and Maintenance Material Management, United States Navy
- 2000, Consolidated Hazardous Material Reutilization & Inventory Management Program, United States Navy
- 2000, Hazardous Material Inventory Control Systems Technician, United States Navy
- 1996, Leadership Development, United States Navy

Memberships and Affiliations

- 2011 – 2012, Student Advisory Board, Strayer University, Washington, DC
- 2007 – Present, Member, Alpha Chi National College Honor Society

Community Service and Leadership

- 2017 – Present, Urban Promise, Mentor, Inner-city high schooler
- 2009 – 2010, Team Helping Hands, Mentor to junior and senior high school student athletes.

Professional and Scholarly Presentations

- 06/16, Business Process, The Boeing Company, Ridley Park, PA
- 12/13, Leadership Theory, University of Phoenix, Phoenix, AZ
- 06/11, Basic APA Writing, Strayer University, Washington, DC

Conferences Attended

2015 & 2016, Ebony Tie Affair, Conference recognizing minority leaders in the community for their contribution to mentoring kids and young teenagers.

Residencies and Colloquia

- 01/13, Doctoral Residency, Creative and Critical Thinking, University of Phoenix
- 12/13, Doctoral Residency, Doctoral Seminar, University of Phoenix
- 11/14, Doctoral Residency, Collaborative Case Study & Doctoral Seminar III, University of Phoenix

Articles and Research

Jackson, K. (2017). *Exploring Perceptions of Mentor Relationships in Doctoral Programs: A Qualitative Exploratory Multiple-Case Study.* Virginia Beach / Richmond, VA: DBC Publishing

Jackson, K. (2016). *Exploring Perceptions of Mentor Relationships in Doctoral Programs: A Qualitative Exploratory Multiple-Case Study.* Dissertation. University of Phoenix, Phoenix, AZ.

Awards and Honors

- 2013, A.T.L.A.S. Award for Supply Chain Performance and Supply Chain Efficiency, Strayer University
- 2007, Summa Cum Laude
- 2005, Magna Cum Laude
- 2005, Navy Commendation Medal
- 1994, 2000, 2001, 2002, Navy Achievement Medal
- 1987, 1989, 1994, 1996, 2002, Naval Supply Efficiency Blue "E" Award

Subject Area Competencies

Software: Microsoft Office Suite, Sales Inventory & Operations Planning (SI&OP), Government Online Data (GOLD)

Learning Management Systems: Blackboard, ICampus, eCampus, D2L

Subject Matter Expert: Management, Strategic Management, Decision Making, Change Management, Organizational Behavior, Human Resources, Educational Management, and Health Services Administration

Personal Attributes

- Extensive professional career training and teaching many military colleagues; highly qualified educator dedicated to excellence in the classroom; ability to efficiently and creatively use experience to address varied learning styles and create relevancy in courses.
- Detail oriented professional with extensive senior level management experience.
- Subject Matter Expert, Supply Chain Manager with expertise in Logistics, Warehousing, Supply Chain Management, and Business Management, and Inventory disciplines.
- Utilize proven teaching strategies that promote student success; apply a variety of teaching styles and adapt instruction to students with diverse learning styles; adept at assessing individual abilities.
- Ability to excel in a demanding, outcome-oriented, and dynamic work environment.
- Effective leader committed to driving results while incorporating lean processes.
- Committed to lifelong learning and seeking new knowledge illustrated by degree attainment.

ABOUT THE AUTHOR

Dr. Kenneth C. Jackson was born and raised in Brooklyn and Queens, New York. He joined the United States Navy, then retired after 21 years of honorable service. He was then hired by The Boeing Company as a Supply Chain Manager responsible for managing and training personnel for logistics, financial accountability, inventory, and material procurement support for V-22's Performance Based Logistics (PBL) Program.

After 11 years of service at The Boeing Company, he was hired by Cecil County, Maryland where he manages and trains personnel for the County's procurement functions adding analytical reviews to complex purchasing requirements.

Dr. Jackson holds an Associate's degree in Business Administration, a Bachelor's degree in Business Administration, a Master's degree in Business Administration, a Master's degree in Education, and a Master's degree in Health Service Administration from Strayer University, and a Doctorate in Management from University of Phoenix. Dr. Jackson is also an online adjunct professor at Montana State University Billing, MT, DeVry University, NY, and Southwestern College, KS. He instructs students in Business and Management disciplines.

He is married to his wife, Tyra, and together have two children and two grandchildren. Dr. Jackson enjoys golfing, officiating college- and high-school basketball, traveling, and spending quality time with family and friends. He also enjoys mentoring youth in his community to bring out the best in those trying to make a difference in themselves.

CONTACT THE AUTHOR
FOR RESEARCH PARTNERING
OR CAREER OPPORTUNITIES

kennethj42867@msn.com

linkedin.com/in/kennethcjackson

ABOUT THE BOOK

The purpose of this qualitative, exploratory, multiple-case study was to explore mentoring relationships and student compatibility in doctoral programs. This design offered and explained an in-depth understanding of what creates a mentor relationship for mentors and doctoral students.

The knowledge gained from this study will assist institutional leaders to focus on continuously developing effective strategies to help bridge the gap of failed mentoring relationships between doctoral candidates and their mentors.

This book is a must read for doctoral chairs, academic deans, and provosts at colleges and universities that have doctoral programs as a guideline to institute, improve, and enhance mentoring relationships between organizational, doctoral-level mentors and doctoral candidate students.

www.ingramcontent.com/pod-product-compliance
Lightning Source LLC
Chambersburg PA
CBHW060022100426
42740CB00010B/1564